R-3944-RC

High Schools with Character

Paul T. Hill, Gail E. Foster, Tamar Gendler

August 1990

PREFACE

This study analyzes big-city high schools: how they function and how the education of the low-income minority youth in these high schools can be improved. It compares comprehensive (or zoned) high schools, special public magnet schools, and Catholic high schools and identifies school features that motivate low-income children to learn and develop into mature adults. Finally, it suggests how these features can be made more broadly available to urban public high school students.

The study was conducted in New York City, and most of its findings apply directly to the improvement of that city's schools. The results also pertain to high school improvement efforts in any major city.

The RAND Corporation supported the study from its own endowment funds. A nonprofit institution conducting research in the public interest, RAND depends on grants and contracts from external sources—principally from government and foundations—to support its research. As in the case of this report, RAND also uses its own endowment funds to support studies on topics of public importance. The immediate audience for the report includes people in New York City—both inside and outside the public school system—intent on making secondary education more effective. The extended audience includes people in other cities concerned with improving high schools for inner-city youth.

SUMMARY

Most people agree that private and special public schools have done a good job of educating minority youth, but most assume that a public school system cannot reproduce that kind of schooling for all of its students. This report shows, to the contrary, that school systems can make the key features of private and special public schools available to all students, and that such schools can work for even the most disadvantaged.

Public high schools in urban areas are among the most troubled and unsuccessful educational institutions in the United States. As a result of low achievement, dropping out, and educational failures, fewer than half of all urban minority children earn diplomas, and many graduate poorly prepared for work or higher education.

Many do not fail, however. Some urban high schools, both public and private, educate and graduate the vast majority of the low-income minority students they enroll. Most such schools enjoy real advantages over typical urban public schools, including freedom from regulation and the ability to enroll only students who genuinely want to attend that school. But these advantages do not tell the entire story: Catholic schools, and special-purpose public schools committed to teaching special skills or providing alternatives to the neighborhood high schools, also operate very differently from the comprehensive (or zoned) urban public high school.

Might students who now attend regular public schools be better motivated and learn more if their schools were more like these special public and Catholic schools? Could the style of education now available only to a few students in such schools be made available to all urban public school students? These issues motivated this study.

Clearly, no study can demonstrate that one kind of school is best for all students. The differences among schools, particularly in parent, student, and teacher motivation, do not permit unambiguous comparisons. We would have no way, short of a controlled experiment, of knowing whether special-purpose public or parochial schools could produce the same outcomes with all public school students that they achieve with their present self-selected student bodies.

Some Catholic and special-purpose public schools serve students whose backgrounds, abilities, and motivations resemble those of typical urban minority public school students. In particular, the New York City Student-Sponsor Partnership Program pays tuition for New York City students in inner-city Catholic high schools. The program aids students from disadvantaged environments. Most scholarship recipients are black or Puerto Rican and many are not Catholic. They tend to come from single-parent welfare homes and have poor scholastic records.

Parochial and special-purpose public schools serving such students face some of the same problems that typical public schools face. We hoped, by observing the operation of such schools, to understand how they motivate and teach. Once we understood that, we sought to examine how the New York public school system could develop high schools with similar features and test their effectiveness with disadvantaged urban students.

METHODS

We studied 13 schools, eight intensively and five partially. All of the schools were located in inner-city neighborhoods and drew from a pool of seriously disadvantaged youths. The zoned comprehensive schools enrolled the largest proportions of poor minority students. But 40 percent of the enrollment in Catholic schools came from families on welfare or living below official poverty thresholds.

The eight schools were in New York City; of the five additional schools, three were in Washington, D.C., and two in New York City. Of the eight, three were Catholic high schools, two were regular neighborhood (zoned) New York City high schools, and two were unique public schools that provided specially focused vocational or academic programs for a cross section of New York City students. Finally, one was a special school designed for students who had failed in regular high schools and were assigned there for a "last chance" at education.

We conducted approximately ten person-days of exhaustive observations, interviews, and record searches in each of the eight schools, and three to five days in each of the remaining schools. We interviewed administrators, teachers, guidance counselors, social service workers, and students and observed classes teaching mathematics, English, and science. We also examined student records and left behind a questionnaire for 50 students in each of the 13 schools.

RESULTS

We found more important similarities than differences among Catholic and special-purpose public schools, and we saw dramatic differences between both of these kinds of schools and zoned public schools. For the purposes of analysis we combined Catholic and special-purpose public schools into a single category, which we called *focus* schools, and compared them with zoned public schools. In many ways, the focus schools have the characteristics of the site-managed schools suggested by educational reformers in the 1980s. In fact, urban parochial schools may be the most mature example of site-managed schools in existence.

Focus schools resemble one another, and differ from zoned comprehensive public schools, in two basic ways. First, focus schools have clear uncomplicated missions centered on the experiences the school intends to provide its students and on the ways it intends to influence its students' performance, attitudes, and behavior. Second, focus schools are strong organizations with a capacity to initiate action in pursuit of their missions, to sustain themselves over time, to solve their own problems, and to manage their external relationships.

Focus schools need not be distinctive or highly innovative. Their organizational independence means, however, that students and staff in each focus school consider their school special, a unique creation that reflects their efforts and meets their needs.

Zoned public schools, in contrast, have diffuse missions defined by the demands of external funders and regulators. They are also profoundly compromised organizations, with little capacity to initiate their own solutions to problems, define their internal character, or manage their relationships with external audiences. Because zoned schools are essentially franchises reflecting a standard model established by central authorities, staff and students have less reason to consider the schools uniquely their own.

The broad categories of mission and organizational strength include other, more specific features that both distinguish focus schools from zoned comprehensive schools and explain the focus schools' particular strengths in educating disadvantaged minority students. Under the category of school mission, the critical differences include the following:

- Focus schools concentrate on *student outcomes* before all other matters. Zoned schools focus primarily on delivering programs and following procedures.
- Focus schools have *strong social contracts* that communicate the reciprocal responsibilities of administration, students, and teachers and establish the benefits that each derives from fulfilling the contract faithfully. Zoned schools try whenever possible to let staff and students define their own roles in the school.

- Focus schools have a *strong commitment to parenting* and aggressively mold student attitudes and values; they emphasize the secular ethics of honesty, reliability, fairness, and respect for others. Zoned schools see themselves primarily as transmitters of information and imparters of skills.
- Focus schools have *centripetal curricula* that draw all students toward learning certain core skills and perspectives. Zoned schools distinguish among students in terms of ability and preference and offer profoundly different curricula to different groups.

Under the broad category of organizational strength and resilience, the critical differences include the following:

- Focus schools operate as *problem-solving organizations*, taking the initiative to change their programs in response to emerging needs. External mandates and rigid internal divisions of labor constrain the problem-solving capability of zoned schools.
- Focus schools *protect and sustain their distinctive character*, both by attracting staff members who accept the school's premises and by socializing new staff members. Zoned schools have little capacity to select staff or influence the attitudes or behavior of new staff members.
- Focus schools consider themselves *accountable to the people who depend on their performance*—parents, students, neighborhood and parish groups, and financial supporters. Zoned schools answer primarily to bureaucratic superiors—outside rule-making, auditing, and assessment organizations.

Table S.1 compares outcomes for three groups of 1989–1990 seniors in the schools that we studied: zoned, special-purpose public, and Catholic schools. Students in the focus schools graduate at a much higher rate than students in zoned schools. The vast majority of graduating seniors in the focus schools take the scholastic aptitude test (SAT), which is required for entry into selective colleges or universities; less than one-third of the graduating seniors in zoned schools take the SAT.

The SAT scores differ profoundly. The scores of the zoned school students fall far below national and focus school averages. Based on the mean scores and distributions provided by the New York City Board of Education, we calculated that only 4 percent of SAT takers in the zoned schools had scores above the national average.

Test scores of students from special-purpose public schools approached the national mean for black students, and Catholic school

Table S.1

COMPARATIVE SAT SCORES OF GRADUATING SENIORS
IN ZONED, SPECIAL-PURPOSE, AND CATHOLIC
SCHOOLS, 1990

Schools	Percentage Graduating	Percentage Taking SAT	Average Combined SAT Score	Percentage Above Mean for Blacks[a]
Zoned public[b]	55	33	642	<30
Special public[b,c]	66	>50	715	>40
Catholic[d]				
Partnership students	82	85	803	>60
All students	95	85	815	>60

[a]Estimates of the proportion of students in each school scoring above the mean for black students are calculated from national SAT norms provided by the Educational Testing Service.
[b]The New York City Board of Education provided the data.
[c]The data do not include seniors in special-purpose public schools for students who had failed in zoned schools. The excluded students tend to be older and more troubled than the average zoned school students and to come from lower-income environments. They graduate at near the average rate for zoned school students, but are unlikely to aspire to a four-year college.
[d]Individual schools and the Partnership Program Office provided the data.

Partnership students comfortably exceeded it. Partnership students in the Catholic schools, many of whom entered below grade level, scored nearly as well as their tuition-paying Catholic school classmates.

Family characteristics and student motivation may explain some of these performance differences. But the conclusion is inescapable: Outcomes for disadvantaged students in focus schools exceeded those for the same students in zoned schools.

IMPLICATIONS

Clearly, the key features of focus schools can be reproduced broadly in public schools, and the vast majority of public school students can profit from schools with those features. In particular:

- The zoned school model has lost its support. Zoned schools are based on decades of interest group negotiation and mandated responses to particular problems. The schools are so encrusted

with rules and procedures that no one in them can work to his or her full potential.
- Near universal dissatisfaction with zoned schools predisposes administrators, teachers, students, and the broader community in favor of dramatic changes.
- Most public school teachers and administrators would prefer to have the freedom and responsibility to solve problems that focus schools have.
- Given the chance, most teachers and administrators would willingly create a social contract in their school and uphold it.
- The vast majority of students now in zoned public high schools would prefer to live under a strong social contract and to be led and guided by adults whom they trust.
- Most inner-city minority students would probably learn more high school language, history, and mathematics if they had the benefit of a focus school's simpler, centripetal curricula.

Focus schools may not work for all students, but they are probably the best form of school for the vast majority of students now served by New York City's zoned comprehensive high schools.

We show how the New York City school system, and those of other major cities, can act now to develop focus schools and make them available to all students. For systems reluctant to commit to full-scale implementation, we also discuss ways to develop and test focus schools on a relatively small scale.

A school system that wants to make focus schools available to all its students must answer these questions:

- Who has to agree to the widespread development of focus schools, and how can they come to agreement?

Parties to the necessary agreement must include the State Department of Education, the superintendent or chancellor, the Board of Education, and the teachers' union. The chancellor should propose the test, suggest its outline, and provide a forum for public discussion.

- What do they have to agree to and what must they avoid?

They have to agree to permit schools to manage themselves. All parties must agree to consider waiving rules and policies that prove to be serious impediments to site management and to act on the results if, after a fair test, the results are favorable. The chancellor and others must avoid trying to reform zoned schools by searching for new standard curricula, general policies controlling school programs, carrot-

and-stick incentives controlled by data systems, and exposés of the failures of individual teachers and principals. Improvement of an organization that has been crushed by regulation, contracts, artificial incentive schemes, and reporting requirements cannot be accomplished by more of the same.

- How can focus schools be created?

Focus schools are site managed, but with a difference. Most site-management schemes transfer the politics of interest group bargaining from the school district to the school building. A focus school, in contrast, is built around specific educational and ethical principles, not around accommodating the interests of all parties. Because existing zoned schools are diverse and fragmented by design, strong agreements on principle are unlikely to emerge within them. Focus schools are best developed from the ground up, around a small core of committed individuals, not by superimposing procedural templates on existing zoned schools. In particular:

— Focus schools must be constructed by the staff members who will work in them.
— Some a priori demonstrations of good faith from principals and lead teachers are required.
— Students and staff members must be able to sort themselves among focus schools and between focus and other schools. Choice will not create focus schools, but it is an indispensable part of a focus-based educational reform.
— Though most focus schools should aim to serve a cross section of city high school students, some schools should target students who have failed in other settings.
— A period of organizational trial and error is essential.
— In dealing with focus schools, the central office must facilitate school-level problem solving, not function as a regulator or evaluator.
— Focus schools must be built one by one, not mass-produced as identical versions of a fixed model.

- How can educators and the public judge whether focus schools are developing properly and helping their students?

The focus school concept should be judged on feasibility and student benefit. The key test of feasibility is simply whether focus public schools can, indeed, develop, recruit, and socialize the staff they need, and serve a true cross section of the city school population. The ultimate criterion is student benefit, i.e., whether disadvantaged minority students attend regularly, experience fewer disciplinary or behavioral problems, graduate in high numbers, take challenging classes, enter institutions of higher education in higher numbers, and score better on consequential standardized tests like the SAT.

- How could a skeptical school system attempt a small test?

A test could be small, initially involving three to ten high schools. It should last long enough for schools to be able to define their individual characters, stabilize staff and curriculum, and have measurable effects on students. Focus schools developed for the test should be designed to fit into the normal funding for the city's public high schools.

Focus schools should meet the tests described above with regard to character stability; attraction and retention of staff; attraction of a cross section of the district population, including a cross section of students now served by zoned high schools in low-income areas; and the ability to serve those students better than do the current zoned schools. Finally, the superintendent, board, teachers' union, and other parties interested in reform—particularly the business community—should agree in advance that the test will be given a fair chance to succeed and the results, if positive, will be acted on.

CONCLUSION

Two related reforms now being urged—choice and site-based management—address real problems. But without an effort to build focus schools, neither choice nor site-based management will dramatically improve inner-city schools.

Site-based management enables a staff to tailor a school to the specific needs of students in attendance; but when given the freedom to govern themselves, staffs of existing schools too often bog down in negotiations about their own working conditions. Choice ensures that staff and teachers can leave schools that they do not like, but it does not guarantee that demand will elicit a supply of good schools, especially in inner cities. With the addition of the focus school concept and its emphasis on a clearly articulated mission combined with institutional integrity, choice and site-based management become powerful engines for the reform of inner-city schools.

Choice and the deregulation that accompanies site-based management create the external conditions for effective schools. But the internal conditions—developing a coherent school mission and the individual character that appeals to students and teachers—matter equally. The effort to develop the internal conditions must be made, not brushed aside as a detail that will be taken care of by the operations of free markets or the professionalism of newly empowered school staffs. The focus school approach shows how schools themselves can become institutions that motivate, lead, and teach disadvantaged inner-city youth.

ACKNOWLEDGMENTS

We are indebted to the hundreds of teachers, students, and administrators in New York City and Washington, D.C., public and Catholic schools who took part in this study. We tried to avoid interfering with the process of schooling, but our presence in offices, hallways, and classrooms inevitably burdened the people who must work and learn there. We are also grateful to the central office administrators of the New York City public and Catholic school systems who gave us access to the schools and offered valuable advice: Victor Herbert, Mary McLaughlin, Barbara Girard, Robert Tobias, James Kearney, and Katherine Hickey.

Peter Flanigan of Dillon, Read & Co., Inc., suggested this study; he and Maggie Ferdon of the New York City Student-Sponsor Partnership Program answered our many questions and helped us throughout. Linda Darling-Hammond of Teachers College, Columbia University, made important suggestions about the study design, as did members of the advisory panel convened by Teachers College President Michael Timpane. Lisa Hudson, Dan Koretz, and Nancy Rizor of RAND helped us analyze and interpret our survey and test data. The reviewers of the report, Bernard Rostker of RAND, James S. Coleman of the University of Chicago, and James Harvey of James Harvey & Associates, greatly improved it.

CONTENTS

PREFACE iii

SUMMARY v

ACKNOWLEDGMENTS xv

TABLES xix

Section
- I. INTRODUCTION 1
  - Origin and Purpose of the Study 1
  - The Schools 3
  - Methods 4
  - Study Design 5
  - Report Structure 5
- II. THE EDUCATIONAL IMPERATIVE: IMPROVING URBAN SECONDARY SCHOOLS 7
  - Significance of Urban Secondary Schools 7
  - Basic Problems of Urban Secondary Schools 8
- III. SCHOOLS' RESPONSE 13
  - How Schools Function 14
  - Composite Catholic High School 15
  - Composite Zoned High School 21
  - Composite Special-Purpose School 26
  - Results 31
- IV. TRANSFORMING PHILOSOPHY INTO COHERENT INSTRUCTION 34
  - Focus Schools Concept 34
  - Mission 36
  - Organizational Strength 47
  - Conclusions 53
- V. THE CASE FOR FOCUS SCHOOLS 57
  - Irreproducible Features 57
  - Student Body Differences 59
  - Desirability 61
  - Feasibility of Implementing Focus Schools 67

VI.	RECOMMENDATIONS AND CONCLUSION	72
	Focus Schools for All	72
	A More Cautious Approach	80
	Conclusion	81

Appendix: STUDENT SURVEY PROCEDURES AND RESULTS 83

STUDENT SURVEY 89

BIBLIOGRAPHY 93

TABLES

S.1.	Comparative SAT scores of graduating seniors in zoned, special-purpose, and Catholic schools, 1990	ix
1.	Demographics of the schools surveyed	9
2.	Key features of schools by type	15
3.	Comparative SAT scores of graduating seniors in zoned, special-purpose, and Catholic schools, 1990	32
4.	Student attitudes toward school and school conditions	65
A.1.	Size and characteristics of survey sample, by school type	83
A.2.	Mean responses to school survey, by school type	84

I. INTRODUCTION

Virtually everyone who will read this report attended high school. Most will view the issue of urban school improvement through the lens of personal experience. But that experience probably bears little resemblance to the reality of urban secondary schools today.

In entering the world of today's urban high school, one must leave outdated assumptions behind. Some may believe that urban public secondary schools provide the only hope for the future or the major impediment to student progress; others may understand parochial high schools as models to be emulated, or as enclaves of the privileged; alternative or magnet schools may be thought of as public education at its best, or at its worst. All of these perceptions, including their internal contradictions, hold true in some respects. But not one of them is wholly accurate, and perceptions based on a school experience of 20 or more years ago hopelessly misrepresent what is going on in each of these schools today.

This report examines why some schools appear to work well, while others drift aimlessly from year to year. It explores the underlying assumptions and working strategies behind the efforts of different schools to respond to the needs of their students. It defines the bargain each school makes with its students. It focuses on how schools motivate students to study and learn.

The report begins by describing the students that these schools serve and the problems that they bring with them to the classroom. It examines the culture of three different kinds of secondary school—church-run, special-purpose public, and zoned comprehensive—and how that culture is reflected in the mission and operations of the schools. It concludes by suggesting how to extend the central features of parochial and special-school practice throughout urban secondary schools or, alternatively, mount limited demonstrations to test the conclusions of this report.

ORIGIN AND PURPOSE OF THE STUDY

The initial impetus for this study came from the Student-Sponsor Partnership Program, which pays tuition so that some low-income New York City students can attend religiously affiliated high schools. Several inner-city private high schools participate in the program; six are Catholic and one is Lutheran. Under the program, often referred to as the Partnership Program, well-to-do New Yorkers of all religious persuasions cover the tuition costs for about 350 low-income African-American and Puerto Rican students who would otherwise attend public schools. The sponsors often help students in public elementary schools who are failing or in danger of dropping out of school and who are of average or below-average ability.

Students in the program are guaranteed tuition in one of the participating schools. They must agree only to attend the school and to work at meeting whatever academic requirements the school establishes. Most come from single-parent homes and subsist on public assistance, and many are not Catholic. Most enter high school two or more years below grade level and score below average on school placement tests. A few score below the tenth percentile. The study was interested in starting with these students because they offered the opportunity to examine how low-income minority students fared in nonpublic schools.

Originally, the study team sought to learn if and how parochial schools succeeded with these students and to compare the experiences of Partnership students with those of students enrolled in zoned comprehensive public schools. As the study progressed, we realized that some magnet and other special-purpose public schools were also experiencing considerable success with low-income minority youngsters. We expanded the scope of the study because this emerging new evidence deserved attention. The focus of the study extended, therefore, to incorporate the experiences of low-income youngsters in these three different kinds of schools.

By reputation, some secondary schools—Catholic schools and special-purpose and magnet public schools—are succeeding with many of the students the typical public school fails to reach, educating and graduating large numbers of urban minority youngsters prepared for the demands of further education, training, or work.

This inquiry set out to examine how these schools succeed and to understand if the typical public school could adapt some of their methods. It examines three different kinds of schools: Catholic schools (also called parochial or religious schools in the text), which many believe are doing an exceptional job; special-purpose public schools (including some magnet schools), which rely on public funds but develop distinctive approaches to serving disadvantaged students; and zoned public high schools, which provide comprehensive educational services to students living in defined geographical areas.

Many others have examined the success of particular types of schools, particularly parochial schools. These studies have been marked by disagreement about whether the results are a function of the school's actions or its selectivity.

The inquiry described here differs from most recent studies. We approach the issue not by examining indicators of student performance and trying to explain the differences, but by going into different kinds of schools to learn how they operate, how they express and realize their expectations of students, what school leaders think they are trying to accomplish, and how they relate to constituencies outside the school building, including parents and outside funding agencies, as well as district administrators, parish priests, school boards, and others higher in the bureaucratic hierarchy.[1]

insights into how each of the three kinds of schools works as an institution. The conclusions consider whether individual features of religious and special-purpose public schools might be adapted to help improve the comprehensive public secondary school. We do not, however, try to make a case for magnet schools or for religious education, but rather to understand how the best ideas from these schools might help to improve educational opportunity for minority youngsters in urban high schools.

THE SCHOOLS

A research team of three people studied 13 schools in the course of this study. It examined eight New York City schools in depth and conducted partial observations in five others, three in Washington, D.C., and two in New York City. Of the eight studied in depth, three were parochial high schools, two were comprehensive New York City public high schools, and three were unique public schools that provided specialized vocational or academic programs for children from throughout the city. Of the unique public schools, two were open to a cross section of all students and one was designed for students who had failed in comprehensive schools, owing to academic, attendance, or behavioral problems.

Throughout this report the unique public schools are referred to as *special-purpose* schools. For variety, they are occasionally called magnet schools, although we exclude selective magnet schools, such as the Bronx High School of Science, from the group. Most of these specialized programs were created in the past decade, although New York City has a long history of supporting specialized trade schools. In some

---

[1]For vivid reports of Catholic school operation, see Margaret M. Camarena, "A Comparison of the Organizational Structures of Public and Catholic High Schools," dissertation, Stanford University, August 1986; James G. Cibulka et al., *Inner City Private Elementary Schools*, Marquette University Press, Milwaukee, 1982; and Janet M. Hudolin, "The Social Organization of an Urban Catholic School: Policy Implications for Public Schools," master's thesis, University of Michigan, August 1989.

ways, as this analysis indicates, the special-purpose schools resemble Catholic schools; in others, they look much more like comprehensive public schools. Some of these special-purpose schools regularly produce student results that match or exceed those of parochial schools.

The Catholic schools studied include only archdiocesan or parochial high schools that admit a cross section of inner-city students; highly selective, college-preparatory Catholic high schools are not part of the analysis. The archdiocesan or parochial high schools—many of them established at the turn of the century to respond to what Catholic parents perceived to be religious intolerance in the public schools—were created to serve Catholic students, largely without regard to academic ability. In recent years, their character has changed: Increasingly, they enroll students from non-Catholic backgrounds and require minimal admission and placement tests.

The zoned public high schools studied were located in low-income neighborhoods and served populations consisting almost entirely of minorities. At our request, the New York City Board of Education nominated schools for the study that were in the middle range of inner-city schools. The two that we visited were considered improving schools: Their academic and student safety records had improved measurably within the past five years and were now considered roughly typical of inner-city zoned high schools.

METHODS

The schools accepting Partnership students agreed to let us spend several days observing classes, reviewing student records, and interviewing administrators, counselors, teachers, and students. Thanks to the generous cooperation of the late Chancellor Richard Green and the New York City Board of Education Division of High Schools, we had comparable access to the students and programs of city public high schools, both zoned comprehensive and special purpose.

Researchers spent about ten person-days in each of the eight schools studied in depth and three to five person-days in the five other schools. The time was spent interviewing the principal and senior administrative staff, observing about ten classes, and conducting approximately 50 additional interviews with students, counselors, and teachers in each school. The team also left behind a detailed attitude questionnaire, to be completed by 50 students in each school.

This intensive data collection provided the study with a rich picture of each school's mission, values, programs, and relationships with students and external groups. The interviews, questionnaires, and observations became the raw material for a detailed case narrative that served as the basis for comparing the schools in this report.

STUDY DESIGN

The study was designed to achieve the following:

- Enable us to understand the three types of schools well enough to know in some detail how they operate as organizations, teaching institutions, and academic and social experiences for students.
- Support an analysis—based on data from the three types of schools—of the distinctive features of Catholic and special-purpose public schools that help to explain their particular effectiveness in serving disadvantaged minority students.
- Explore the organizational and personnel incentives that allow schools to implement and sustain those key features.
- Formulate hypotheses about how these features could be created in regular public schools and suggest how the hypotheses could be fully implemented on a broad scale—or tested on a smaller scale—if doing so would make any discernible difference to the larger school population.

We then moved beyond the analyses of data to ask: How can the key features of Catholic and special-purpose schools be made more broadly available in public schools? What actions, including funding, training, and changes in regulations and contracts, would be necessary? These questions provided the analytical backbone for the sections that follow.

REPORT STRUCTURE

Section II outlines the importance of improving urban secondary schools and describes the educational problems of inner-city high school students. The third section presents composite profiles of the three kinds of schools that we studied—Catholic, special-purpose public, and zoned public—and examines student performance. The profiles provide the basic facts used in later analysis.

Section IV analyzes the principal differences among the schools that we studied, highlighting critical similarities and differences in mission, organization, management of student life, curriculum, and instruction. It concludes with a set of summary statements about the features of

Catholic and special-purpose public schools that set them apart from comprehensive public high schools and appear to make them particularly effective in serving students.

The fifth section addresses the question of generalizability: What evidence do we have that the features that we have identified could be adapted or reproduced in comprehensive public schools, and what is the evidence that such features would improve student and school performance? The final section explores the implications of what we have found and shows how school systems can create focus schools and assess their effectiveness for disadvantaged students.

II. THE EDUCATIONAL IMPERATIVE: IMPROVING URBAN SECONDARY SCHOOLS

Urban public secondary schooling is the embarrassing secret hidden in the nation's educational closet. Despite the ceaseless clamor of the past decade about school performance in the United States—much of it directed toward secondary schools—only a few analysts and policy initiatives have focused specifically on the needs of urban schools, and these have dealt almost invariably with the needs of urban children in the preschool and early elementary years.

SIGNIFICANCE OF URBAN SECONDARY SCHOOLS

If the nation's larger educational agenda is to be met, and if the needs of a large and expanding minority student population are to be addressed, the effort must start in the nation's cities. In New York State, for example, 41 percent of the students enrolled in public schools can be found in only five city school systems: the boroughs of New York City, along with Buffalo, Rochester, Syracuse, and Yonkers.[1] These five cities also enroll 82 percent of the state's minority students (black, Hispanic, native American, and Asian or Pacific islander).[2] Almost all of the state's language-minority students live in these five urban areas, most of them in New York City.[3]

New York City itself enrolls 36 percent of all the public school students in the state and three out of four of the state's minority students. In addition, the *city*'s nonpublic school enrollment represents 11 percent of the *state*'s total public school enrollment.[4] Whatever the problems of the state's suburban and rural schools—and the problems are very real—the state cannot possibly hope to improve statewide student performance or the overall quality of its labor force without marked improvement in the big-city schools now enrolling nearly half of all public school students. And that goal depends first and foremost on turning around the public schools of New York City.

---

[1] State Education Department, *New York, The State of Learning: Statewide Profile of the Educational System*, Albany, New York, January 1, 1989, Table 4A.
[2] Ibid., Table 5.
[3] Ibid., Table 6.
[4] Ibid., Table 4A.

If the effort is to start in urban areas, then it must take root in the early years. Existing analytical and policy attention to preschool and elementary education is clearly a sensible first step. But genuine reform cannot succeed unless urban secondary schools receive simultaneous attention. It is during the high school years that the deficiencies in school and nonschool support for urban youngsters, particularly minority youngsters, have such brutal consequences for the students, their families, and their communities.

In the secondary school years, academic and behavioral problems that were manageable with children in the early grades become overwhelming as students mature and have to deal with the more complicated demands of high school mathematics and language. Economic and neighborhood decay that could be kept partly at bay in the child's formative years become central to the high school student's experience. The routine demands of school confront the excitement of adolescence and the heady income possibilities of an open underground economy. As a result, while community leaders blame the school and school personnel point to the community, absenteeism increases, achievement declines, and maintaining order in the school overrides academic progress.

Many families try to cope with the difficulties by pretending that nothing is wrong. This approach imposes an enormous long-term strain on everyone involved. Others try to bring the problem into the open, discuss it, and examine alternative ways to proceed. Experts agree that, despite the initial stress involved, this approach promises stronger and healthier families in the long run. The analysis in subsequent sections of this report is designed to bring the problem into the open so that it can be discussed and examined as a first step in creating stronger and healthier schools.

BASIC PROBLEMS OF URBAN SECONDARY SCHOOLS

Because they are located in inner-city neighborhoods and serve low-income minority students, the three kinds of schools described in this study draw from a pool of seriously disadvantaged youth. Table 1 displays broad demographic data about the students in these schools.

As the data indicate, both the Catholic and special-purpose public schools can be relatively small (500 to 600 students), but schools as large as 2400 to 2600 are found in each group. Zoned schools were all large. Both types of public school were much more heavily staffed by teachers, administrators, and support personnel than the Catholic schools.

Table 1

DEMOGRAPHICS OF THE SCHOOLS SURVEYED

Student Characteristics	Zoned Public	Special-Purpose Public	Catholic
Percentage of students who are			
Hispanic	60	50	49
Black	40	40	25
White	0	5	25
Asian	0	5	1
Percentage with families on welfare or in poverty	75	40	40
Percentage with parents who completed high school[a]	56	86	69
School size range	1800–2400	500–2600	600–2500
Student-to-staff ratio	11:1	11:1	20:1
Percentage of students admitted below grade level	65–75	25–40	35

[a]From student survey; see the appendix.

In terms of minority poverty, zoned comprehensive schools enroll the largest proportion of poor black and Hispanic students. Enrollment in such schools consists entirely of minority students, three-quarters of them from families on public assistance and at least two-thirds of them below grade level. Substantial numbers of students in each of the other two types of school are also low-income minorities: Between 75 and 90 percent of students in Catholic and special-purpose schools are black and Hispanic, 40 percent of them on public assistance, but only one-third are below grade level.

Students in all of the schools in this study come from neighborhoods—in the Bronx, Brooklyn, and Manhattan—with formidable problems. Some come from neighborhoods in which crime and public health statistics are, quite literally, among the worst in the world. Four schools—two zoned, one Catholic, and one special purpose—draw at least a few students from the Harlem neighborhoods where male life expectancy is lower than that in Bangladesh.[5] Many of the children in these schools exhibit severe health problems resulting from poor prenatal care, inadequate nutrition, untreated infections, and exposure to lead paint and other toxic materials. Many are exposed to

---

[5]See Colin McCord, M.D., and Harold P. Freeman, M.D., "Excess Mortality in Harlem," *New England Journal of Medicine*, Vol. 33, No. 3, January 18, 1990, pp. 173–177.

molds in dilapidated buildings; in one zoned school, children suffer from asthma due to exposure to molds in the school itself.

In those neighborhoods more than half of all children are born out of wedlock. The majority of children in the schools studied live with only one parent—many lived with grandparents, with more remote relatives, or in group homes. As many as 25 percent of the children in these neighborhoods become parents before they reach the normal high school graduation age of 18.

In short, each of the eight schools studied is struggling to cope with the problems of urban decay and social disintegration. Some children in all the schools studied, including the Catholic schools, had recently been convicted or charged with criminal activities. Dozens were in protective custody to escape violence from parents, older siblings, or parents' companions. Principals in every school had banned beepers because many students were using them to arrange drug sales.

Catholic school principals were particularly concerned that school uniforms were used as protective cover by students dealing drugs, as students wearing them were less likely to be questioned by police. Three of the schools in this study (one Catholic, one special-purpose public, and one zoned public) served students whose brothers had been charged in the infamous Central Park "wilding" attacks on joggers in 1989. During our study the parents of several students in one Catholic school were indicted for extortion and murder.

Language

In addition to these environmental problems, approximately one-sixth of the students in our schools are recent immigrants, mostly from Puerto Rico or from Latin American countries. Many have had little formal schooling, and most exhibit moderate to severe problems reading and speaking English. Though some Spanish-speaking students become fluent English speakers, most are handicapped throughout high school by their unfamiliarity with written English and idiom. Because most use English only with other students, they have difficulty attaining an adult level of English proficiency.

Motivation

Although they grow up in one of the world's great commercial and cultural centers, many children in New York's inner-city neighborhoods have little interest—and perceive themselves as having no stake—in the larger society. Because many immigrant students come from very poor rural areas, they often succumb to the lure of low-wage jobs. They can usually earn enough to enjoy a higher level of consumption than adults in their home villages enjoyed and therefore see little need for continued education.

Native-born students in these schools are also attracted by jobs in both the legal and underground economies. Many are tempted to drop out to work full-time; those who work part-time often have little time for study and are too weary to pay full attention in classes. These are the classic unmotivated urban high school students for whom jobs and the other distractions of adolescence can overpower anything the schools have to offer.

Some parents manage to keep their children focused on the importance of schooling. But few have the time or the knowledge required to participate in their children's education. Even the parents who work to put their children into private or public magnet schools take a passive approach to education, and most can only hope that the schools can find a way to motivate their children. If the school fails in that effort, the students are unlikely to develop the attendance patterns and discipline that they need to master high school material. Motivating the unmotivated constitutes the first challenge of all the schools in this study.

Dropouts

As one result of these problems, the high schools do not even see some of the children who are promoted to ninth grade. Nearly 10 percent disappear after junior high school (eighth grade for most New York City students, ninth grade for a few). Some simply evade authorities; others legally drop out because their academic progress was so slow they had turned 16 before leaving the eighth grade.

Of the students who actually enroll in high school, slightly more than one-half are likely to gain a regular high school diploma. In 1987-1988, 140,000 students were registered in public high schools in Brooklyn, the Bronx, and Manhattan. If one in four had graduated that year, the total number of graduates would have been 35,000. In fact, only 22,000 graduated—63 percent of the number that would routinely be expected.

These numbers include selective high schools open to all students citywide. Throughout the city, in zoned schools open to all, less than 55 percent of the expected number of students graduated.[6] Some of the students not graduating from regular high schools later pursue General

---

[6]New York City Board of Education, Office of Research, Evaluation, and Assessment, *Accountability Section Report: The Annual Dropout Rate 1987-88*, 1989.

Education Diplomas and other credentials. But when most of the students in such programs enroll, they are already burdened with children and heavy financial obligations.

III. SCHOOLS' RESPONSE

Many reformers have urged public school change in response to the problems described in the preceding section. Many of these recommendations, particularly in the earliest stages of the reform movement, demanded more rigor, stronger curriculum content, and greater accountability for results in secondary schools.[1]

More recently, school reformers have turned their attention to the importance of creating schools—both elementary and secondary—that can function as self-sustaining, problem-solving organizations.[2] These later reforms emphasize the importance of site-based management so as to make the school a community characterized by strong internal bonds and a capacity for influencing all of its members— administrators, teachers, staff, students, and parents. Much of this discussion depends on theory about organizational behavior, with illustrations drawn from corporate experience or from exemplary school efforts thought to embody the principles of site management.

Several spokesmen and researchers have cited the initial reform focus on standards and accountability as inimical to the interests of minority children.[3] More recently, however, various site-based management strategies have been harnessed to the improvement of educational opportunities for minority youngsters. Minority leaders increasingly argue that greater school autonomy to meet the particular needs of youngsters in each school can benefit all students and, in particular, students from minority backgrounds.[4]

---

[1]See, for example, National Commission on Excellence in Education, *A Nation at Risk: The Imperative for Educational Reform*, Washington, D.C., 1983; also U.S. Department of Education, *American Education: Making It Work*, Washington, D.C., 1988.

[2]See, for example, Ronald R. Edmonds, "Making Public Schools Effective," *Social Policy*, September-October 1981, pp. 56-60; John I. Goodlad, *A Place Called School: Prospects for the Future*, McGraw-Hill, New York, 1984, p. 229; Carnegie Institution, *A Nation Prepared*, Forum on Education and the Economy, Washington, D.C., 1986; James P. Comer, "Educating Poor Minority Children," *Scientific American*, Vol. 259, No. 5, November 1988, pp. 42-48; and Albert Shanker, "Restructuring American Education," in *Roundtable on Urban Education*, Business-Higher Education Forum, Washington, D.C., 1989.

[3]See, for example, Daniel Koretz, "Arriving in Lake Wobegon: Are Standardized Tests Exaggerating Achievement and Distorting Instruction?" *American Educator*, Summer 1988, pp. 8-15.

[4]See Massachusetts Institute of Technology, *Education That Works: An Action Plan for the Education of Minorities*, Quality Education for Minorities Project, Cambridge, 1990.

Few proposals—whether from the general reform movement or from those most concerned with the education of minority teenagers—have considered how schools outside regular public school systems work with low-income minority students. Nor have they considered the possibility that special-purpose public and religiously affiliated schools are, in fact, models of the very schools their proposals advocate. But, as the analysis in this document concludes, one striking similarity between special-purpose public schools and Catholic schools is that they are both site managed.

Special-purpose public schools turn out to be unique creations of their administration and staff. Individual Catholic schools are even more independent, essentially managing their own affairs, except when they need occasional help from a minuscule central bureaucracy. The diocesan schools in New York and other major cities may, indeed, be the most mature and solidly established example of what a school system based on site management looks like.

HOW SCHOOLS FUNCTION

Site-management advocates insist that each school be understood as a distinct organization. Without knowing the school's style of operation and the ways in which school personnel characteristically behave and think, reform advocates cannot plausibly predict the consequences of the proposals they put forward.

This section describes Catholic, comprehensive (or zoned), and special-purpose public schools as the research team observed them in the 1989–1990 school year, in terms of demographics and student enrollment, mission, curriculum, and accountability relationships. It concludes with a summary of student achievement. Taking this description a step further, Sec. IV examines the interplay between the schools' formal positions—as reflected in such things as statements of mission and curricula—and their habits, customs, and strategies for dealing with educational problems.

Rather than trying to describe the dynamics of 13 complex individual schools—thereby imposing an intolerable burden on the reader—we synthesize below three fictional composite schools. We found the synthesis feasible because schools of each kind exhibited a high degree of internal consistency, i.e., they were true to type. This device offers the additional advantage of permitting us to honor our pledge to school personnel not to identify individual schools in our report.

The composites are based on the data collected in three Catholic, two zoned public, and three special-purpose public schools in New

York City. In addition, some secondary elements of the composites are drawn from less extensive fieldwork in other schools in New York City and in Washington, D.C. Table 2 compares key features for each school type.

COMPOSITE CATHOLIC HIGH SCHOOL

Demographics and School Site

Founded 100 years ago by an order of priests, this school today serves 700 boys from around New York City. (The Catholic schools that we studied ranged in size from 600 to 2500.) Once exclusively Irish and Italian Catholic, the school's population today is closer to 65 percent Catholic; approximately one-half of the students are Hispanic, one-quarter are black, and one-quarter are white.

Table 2

KEY FEATURES OF SCHOOLS BY TYPE

	Zoned Public	Special-Purpose Public	Catholic
Mission	Preparation of graduates for higher education, work, citizenship, college entry	Preparation of responsible, reliable, thoughtful graduates for college or semiprofessional career in health care	Preparation of spiritual, educated, mature, independent, responsible adults ready for 4-year college
Curriculum	11 electives; strict tracking	1 or 2 electives; emphasizes health-care training and state graduation requirements	Few electives; little vocational training
Remediation	Through 12th grade	Ends in 10th grade	Ends in 10th grade
Accountability and external relationships	Almost entirely accountable to external control	Self-contained to extent school can avoid state and city requirements	Almost entirely self-contained; little central control

Though the school once served a cohesive parish community, its current clientele is now diverse and dispersed. The student body is drawn from throughout the city; consequently, no broader community defines and protects the school. The school defines itself and creates its own community.

Just over half of the students come from single-parent homes, but most mothers work; two-thirds of the students come from families that find a way to pay at least part of the school's $1900 annual tuition. One-third of the students have scholarships from the New York City Student-Sponsor Partnership Program or other social service agencies. The school keeps some students who have no source of tuition money in the hope that their parents will someday be able to make partial repayments. The school's per pupil expenditure slightly exceeds $3000, with the difference coming from the diocese, fund-raisers, and borrowing.

The school's principal is a 60-year-old priest. Of the 34 teachers, 22 are Catholic, and most went to Catholic high school at some time during their childhood. One-quarter of the teachers are brothers (members of the religious order who are not ordained priests), and three-quarters are members of the laity, including six women. Only one of the teachers is black; two are Hispanic. Most of the brothers are over fifty and have spent 30 or more years in schools run by their religious order. The lay teachers tend to be younger, with a stable core staff in their mid-40s who have been at the school for 15 to 20 years and a more transient group in their 20s and 30s.

The school site is a century-old downtown building, well but simply maintained: The stairs are worn, but safe; the cafeteria cramped, but clean; hall moldings are lined with trophies won by school teams over the decades. The classrooms are simple, decorated with crucifixes and a few posters. During classes, the stairwells and hallways are empty. When classes change, corridors are filled with rambunctious but well-behaved hordes of high school boys in white shirts, green ties, and navy jackets.

Mission

For the past century, the school has devoted itself to educating the sons of the poor and working classes and teaching them to be good Christians, workers, and citizens. In the past 50 years, its mission has also included preparing them for college, and today some 75 percent of its graduates go on to two- and four-year colleges. Most students want to study business at a four-year institution in the New York City area. The school's ideal graduate is "spiritual, educated, mature, independent, and socially responsible," and the school seeks to develop this sort of character in its students through a combination of firm rules and personal attention.

The rules on paper are strict: Cutting classes is punished by detention; being out of uniform results in demerits; talking back to a teacher leads to serious reprimand; and fighting, cheating, or stealing is grounds for expulsion. But disciplinary action is infrequent. Except for minor infractions, students tend to obey the rules. Some 25 boys are asked to stay for detention each day, most for failure to turn in homework rather than for misbehavior.

Although the school has a dean responsible for discipline, all staff members are expected to respond to all violations of school rules and values. The school invariably follows up on minor offenses as a way of keeping order and attending to events in the students' lives. "If a boy gets the three basic rules into place—attendance, lateness, and the dress code," explains the principal, "the rest follows naturally." The principal also notes that small offenses can signal more important problems and cites the example of a student who violated the dress code. The teacher who confronted him learned that the student had been put out of his aunt's house. Subsequently, the school arranged placement in a protective group home.

The school sees itself as carrying a greater burden of regulating students' behavior than it would have if parents were stricter. This is a change from 50 years ago, when school and parents worked in concert to instill values in the students. Today, the school acts as a surrogate (rather than supplementary) authority figure. All of the boys have some adult, whether parent or sponsor, who brought him to the attention of the school and either pays his tuition or arranges to have it paid. But this situation does not guarantee that the values in the boy's home reflect those of the school. In fact, parent-sanctioned truancy has led the principal to ask parents at the annual meeting not to collaborate in their sons' schemes by writing excuse notes. Many of the parents are intimidated by their sons, who are already better educated than themselves. "Remember," the principal admonishes, "you are still the parents, and your children need you to be firm with them."

The school itself has no trouble asserting its authority. It is convinced that what it demands of the boys helps them, and it is willing to take the steps necessary to mold them. It does not assume that students will immediately take to the school's requirements; rather, it views its charges as malleable, full of potential but not fixed in their ways. New students are closely watched, particularly those who come from public schools and to whom the new school's culture is unfamiliar. "They have trouble at first," explains the principal, "actually understanding that when we say 'do your homework,' we mean it. But we prod them; we remind them that they're lucky to be here. And they watch the way the other kids act. They catch on." New students are frequently impressed with the school's consistency: "When they say something here, they mean it. If you don't do your work, they come after you every time."

Teachers are expected to keep track of their students. If a boy is absent, the teacher will often ask the boy's friends where he is. Many teachers serve as informal counselors ("every teacher here is a guidance counselor, whether he wants to be or not," explains the assistant principal), but when a boy has severe problems, the teacher is expected to refer him to a professional ("teachers are not trained psychologists").

Teachers feel no qualms about criticizing students' behavior or asking them to act in a particular way; students and teachers alike have a clear sense that the school's actions are for the students' own good. They also have the sense of school as family. "We try to take the place of what's missing outside," explains the assistant principal: "The secretaries give out Band-Aids; our woman teachers represent mothers; our male teachers represent fathers."

Staff and Teaching

Instruction centers almost entirely on teachers. Although the administration recognizes that lecturing is not the most effective way to teach boys of this age and background, it has few resources for staff development. Because salaries are so low, many younger teachers (who earn $19,000 at entry with the prospect of $35,000 after 15 years) are forced to leave out of financial necessity.

The school tries to overcome these handicaps by offering teachers a warm, supportive place to teach—the most comfortable room in the school is the newly remodeled teachers' lounge—and by selecting faculty on the basis of their commitment to Catholic education and to the population the school serves. But many of the older teachers, particularly the brothers, are frustrated because they have trouble reaching the boys. A new assistant principal is working with older teachers to enliven their classes and incorporate more modern teaching techniques, an effort he expects to take several years.

Despite some tension between the old guard and the younger teachers, the faculty members share a sense of working toward the same end. About three students are expelled each year for disciplinary reasons and another five to ten are asked not to return for academic reasons. The faculty care deeply about the school's students, and many consider giving up on any boy to be a personal failure. In theory and to some extent in practice, the school is committed to treating students as individuals and to valuing the individual over the system.

Organization and Curriculum

Although the school is nominally part of a larger Catholic hierarchy, it is essentially self-contained. Neither the central Catholic school office nor the local pastor has the time or resources to devote much attention to the school. As a result, the school is almost completely free of bureaucratic constraints from above. Aside from the curriculum restrictions imposed by accreditation requirements and the commitment to the basic philosophy of the religious order, the staff are free to solve problems as they see fit. The main limitation comes from lack of resources; some of the programs that might help students require money that the school simply does not have.

Curriculum. The curriculum includes almost no electives. All students take a basic academic schedule of four years of English, religion, and physical education; three years each of social studies and mathematics; two years each of science, art, and foreign language; and one year each of music, health, and computer literacy. Most courses are offered at standard and honors levels; ninth- and possibly tenth-grade classes have remedial tracks as well.

Class time is used efficiently, and teachers are well prepared, but students are rarely asked other than rhetorical or short factual questions. Hands-on learning, with the exception of honors science laboratories, is uncommon. Among students in honors classes, no stigma attaches to doing well, but in the standard track, academic excellence does not make one popular with one's peers. The school has tried to change this norm through awards assemblies and "student of the month" bulletin boards, but thus far it has not succeeded.

Students have homework in most classes every night. Most assignments involve reading the textbook or an original source (e.g., a novel for English class) and preparing to answer oral questions in class. All students have at least one assignment that requires one or two pages of expository writing each week.

Tracking. Boys are placed in tracks according to their standardized test scores and previous records. Most honors students have scores above the 80th percentile, with most other students assigned to the standard track. Tracking assignments are not rigidly fixed, but scheduling difficulties tend to hinder scheduling a boy in, say, remedial mathematics and honors (or even standard) English.

Remedial Work. Boys admitted to the school with skills below the school's minima are required to attend a four-week summer session and take remedial-track courses during the ninth and tenth grades. Virtually all of the students in the Partnership Program are well below grade level when admitted. They—and approximately 20 other students with serious academic deficiencies admitted each year on grants—are required to attend summer school and take remedial classes in ninth grade. The course content of all three tracks is theoretically the same, with differences arising from pacing and depth.

As in most schools, however, the remedial classes emphasize learning of facts over discussion of alternative perspectives. Whereas tenth-grade honors students have laboratories in biology and are expected to learn by reading fiction on their own, remedial students have only a textbook in biology and vocabulary and lessons in English grammar. By eleventh grade, however, the program (with the exception of mathematics) is reduced to the honors and standard tracks, and students from the remedial track attend standard classes. Those who still need help are expected to ask teachers for assistance. The school also runs an afternoon study hall required for students who fail more than one class.

Specialness of the School. The school tries to set itself apart from the world in which most of the boys grow up. The uniform is one manifestation of this: "It instills a sense that school is serious, that education means work," says the principal. Another is the kind of rhetoric that fills assemblies: "You're not in public school any more; you've come here because you want to be better; you have goals."

The boys seem to accept the fact that to benefit from the school they have to play by the rules. Some see it as a simple trade-off—if I follow the rules here, I'll be able to stay with all my friends. Others have internalized it more—if I learn how to act like they want me to, I'll be a better person. Many of the boys have an image of who they would be if they were not at this school. One ninth grader explained: "If I had gone to public school, I'd fool around, hang out late, do no homework, take drugs. Kids at public school—no one really pays attention to them."

Faculty and staff have a highly developed sense of the school's identity. They take the responsibility to students extremely seriously; doing whatever they can is a question of conscience. In its most lofty moments, the school sees itself as entrusted with the souls of 700 boys; in less elevated terms, it feels obligated to the boys' parents and to the tradition of the founding religious order.

The school's warrant for authoritative action stems in large part from its place within the larger tradition of Catholic schools. Parents trust the school because of both the individuals who run it and the legacy it represents. The school, in turn, sees itself as responsible not only to this generation of students and parents, but to both the past and the future of the religious order and Catholic schools in general.

COMPOSITE ZONED HIGH SCHOOL

Demographics and School Site

This high school has traditionally been a port-of-entry school, serving working-class German and Irish immigrants at the turn of the century, and lower-middle-class European Jews from the 1920s to the early 1960s. When the Jewish population moved to the suburbs in the 1960s and 1970s, middle-class black families moved into the district. For the past 20 years the school has been predominantly black and Hispanic; no student of Northern European descent has graduated since 1968.

Until 15 years ago, the student body came from fairly stable homes. But in the late 1970s, owing to the effects of rent control on willingness to maintain buildings, much poorer families moved in and the neighborhood became a center for drugs and crime. Although some neighborhood families have steady working-class incomes, the entire school is considered eligible for Chapter I, the federal compensatory education program for low-income students, and for free lunch.

On a given day, enrollment at the school totals about 2000 (in the 1950s it was 5200), with some 1400 students attending. The number of formal enrollments each year exceeds 3000 because of the high number of transfers in and out of the school area. Some students enroll more than once as they return from visits of varying length to Puerto Rico, the Dominican Republic, or the rural south. Forty percent of all enrollments occur after the school year begins. The school is 60 percent Hispanic and 40 percent black, but owing to the mobility of the Hispanic population, graduates are 60 percent black and 40 percent Hispanic. Three years ago no student received a Regents' Diploma; in spring 1989, 11 students earned that distinction.[5]

Seventy-eight percent of the students are two years below grade level in reading; 65 percent are two years below in computational skills. Twelve percent of the students are in special education; 12 percent are non-English speaking; and 100 are immigrants who can provide no record of prior schooling. Between 150 and 200 students became parents last year.

---

[5]The Regents' Diploma is a mark of distinction for students who successfully complete a rigorous academic program, including foreign language, advanced mathematics, and challenging English and social studies courses.

The principal is a middle-aged Jewish man who has been at the school one year; before that he was assistant principal for administration at a Brooklyn high school. The school has about 180 teachers. Half of the teachers are dedicated loyalists who have made their careers in the school; many are graduates of the school. Half are short-termers who will look for other assignments as soon as they can. Thirty of the teachers are Jewish and 30 Irish; about one-quarter of the younger cohort are black and Hispanic.

The school building is structurally sound and most of the hallways are reasonably clean, lined with construction paper-covered bulletin boards on topics from nutrition to school rings to algebra. The classrooms are less appealing. Plaster falls from many of the ceilings; candy wrappers and soda cans begin collecting under the desks after first period; in the high-ceilinged classrooms, the paint above the 12-foot mark looks as old as the building itself; and student work displayed on classroom bulletin boards is sometimes defaced with graffiti.

Small groups of students lounge in the hallways, often the same students period after period. The hallways appear safe during change of class, but there are reports of students assaulting other students on the back staircase.

To enter the building, students must present a computer-coded badge to a security guard at the door. If a guard finds a knife on a student, the knife is confiscated and a parent is notified. The head of security estimates that 20 to 40 percent of the students carry knives, but they are rarely used, and anyone caught holding a knife inside the building is immediately suspended. There is little evidence of drug use or sales on the school grounds, although a member of the research team did witness an apparent drug transaction in a student lavatory.

Mission

In theory, the school seeks to provide its students with solid academic training that will prepare them for higher education, productive work, and responsible citizenship. But this goal is overshadowed by day-to-day concerns. In practice, the school's basic mission is to meet as many of its students' severe and varied needs as possible through whatever programs it can muster.

Special programs include attendance outreach, parenting classes, ethnic music and art programs, and temporary housing for homeless students. Although the principal would like for these programs to fit coherently into some larger scheme, he cannot keep track of all the pieces. And, he says, "We couldn't simplify the school without neglecting or discriminating against someone."

Although the school nominally anticipates that all students will graduate, few teachers or administrators genuinely expect this to happen. Fewer than 60 percent of the ninth graders are promoted to tenth grade, and by graduation time, only 35 percent to 45 percent of those who started with the class remain. Much of the school's energy is devoted to making these figures look less bleak when reported to the Board of Education—in effect, finding ways to keep students on the rolls until they "age out" at 19.

The school is further fractionated by its division into "houses," which are intended to give the students the feeling of a smaller "home base." But in practice, few students have a sense of commitment to the house to which they are assigned. The houses serve mainly to honor test-score distinctions among entering students, with houses for honors, college-bound (standard track), business, bilingual, and special-education students.

Staff and Teaching

Staff share no coherent, overarching goal. Each is committed to a specific program or organizational unit—an academic department, the health clinic, the newspaper, the job development program, the African dance class—many of which are funded from sources outside the school and to which the staff feel responsible.

Teachers are not expected to serve as counselors. While some teachers have developed a deep personal rapport with their students, others allow the bureaucracy to buffer them from close contact. For instance, a central office handles cutting. Teachers are simply required to keep records for their own classes, which the office combines to create attendance records for each student. Unless the office requests or demands action, many teachers consider record keeping the limit of their responsibility. Teachers inclined to follow up on absenteeism are often prevented from doing so by other, overwhelming demands on their time.

The school has a large number of formal counselors, including two guidance counselors at each grade level, nine family assistants, four social worker/investigators devoted to attendance issues, three visiting social workers from a community-based organization, a dropout-prevention coordinator, a college counselor, a career counselor, a part-time psychologist, and a full-time physician in the on-site health clinic.

Some students establish stable relationships with one or another of the counselors. Others are sent in for ad hoc meetings in response to a particular problem. But many students resist contact by giving the school false addresses and inventing phone numbers, leaving the school at a loss in both disciplinary and counseling cases.

Discipline

Although the school strictly enforces rules governing the most severe behaviors—no fighting, no weapons, no drugs—most less serious violations are tacitly ignored. Despite a sign reading "No Hats or Walkmans," requests to remove these are frequently ignored with no further consequences. Lateness is not punished; in fact, students are given only three minutes between classes, making adherence to the hypothetical rule nearly impossible.

The school seems reluctant to make demands for fear of violating students' rights or driving them away. The school feels compelled to keep as many students as possible in attendance each day, so it is willing to tolerate almost anything as long as it takes place within the building and does not disrupt others. Students are happy to have a warm, safe place to spend the day with their friends and to earn a certificate that may enable them to get a better job.

Teachers and students tacitly agree that life will be most pleasant for both if they keep interference in each other's lives to a minimum. In practice, this works out to be a compact in which adults agree not to demand too much in return for the students' agreement not to cause trouble. Some extraordinary teachers and students rise above the compact—individual classes vary from abysmal to outstanding—but it is a powerful force in the life of the school.

Organization

The school is severely constrained by the regulations and procedures that govern it. The principal, for example, has little authority in hiring staff. Those he is calculated to need are simply assigned by the central office and appear, armed with a contract prohibiting their dismissal, at the school in September. The principal tries to hire good teachers and good permanent substitutes whenever possible and to block any particularly bad new teachers from achieving tenure. But his efforts require tremendous amounts of paperwork, physical and emotional energy, and often fail anyway.

For their part, teachers also face enormous frustrations. Maintaining coherence in academic offerings and stability in student class assignments is very nearly impossible in light of the central office's control of teaching assignments. For example, as the school's average daily attendance declines throughout the year (as students formally drop out or simply stop coming to school), teacher slots are cut and some teachers must abruptly leave the school. Some programs, such as bilingual education, suffer teacher cuts of up to 20 percent in midyear.

Furthermore, many of the external programs from which the school benefits—such as those sponsored by the city and by private foundations—come with numerous requirements that prevent the school from adapting them to its needs or combining them into a larger framework. The lack of resources, contract requirements, city and state regulations, and staff reluctance to work beyond their formal responsibilities all constrain the school's ability to initiate.

Curriculum

To graduate, students must pass the Regents' Competency Tests (RCTs) in reading, writing, mathematics, science, and American and world history, as well as complete four years of English, social studies, and physical education; two years of mathematics and science; one year of foreign language and health; and one semester of art, music, and speech.[6] The remaining 11 of a student's courses are electives.

Although the school remains committed to its academic curriculum, many teachers consider it inappropriate for the current population. They believe that student transience hinders the presentation of a coherent, cumulative program; moreover, some students enter with such low skill levels that many cannot even read on their own.

Classes are strictly tracked, and students have little mobility after freshman year. Honors students—generally those with standardized test scores above the 50th percentile—get the best teachers and stay together in the same small group over the four years. Students with low test scores and grades, as well as behavior problems, are placed in special education classes; about 1 percent graduate.

The caliber and style of instruction vary tremendously among teachers, but opportunities for student input are rare in most classes. Even honors students rarely spend more than an hour per night on homework. Ninth-grade English homework might be: "Write two sentences about a character in the book we are reading."

Students have low academic expectations and learn quickly that doing the bare minimum to earn a diploma will still place them in the ranks of "successes." Failing two classes is considered normal. Cutting, far from the exception, is the rule. During class, students eat, rifle through their purses, comb their hair, sleep, get up and walk around, even leave. On sunny days in the spring, afternoon classes of 25 can expect to draw 5 or 10 students. Honors classes do somewhat better, seldom falling below 50 percent attendance.

---

[6]Regents' Competency Tests, demonstrating minimal academic proficiency, are required of all high school graduates.

External Relationships

The school is accountable largely to outside forces. Its curriculum must meet state standards; its teachers work under union contracts; and its internal structure must conform to city requirements, as must its disciplinary code and its schedule. The administration devotes much of its time to providing various outside groups—the Board of Education, the foundations that have given it money, and state education officials—with statistics showing how much it has improved as a result of particular externally funded projects.

As in the Catholic schools, parents do not share in the school's policy decisions. A small PTA meets occasionally, but most parents are either intimidated by, uninterested in, or incapable of participating in school activities.

The sense of powerlessness that accompanies the school's accountability to outside forces is intensified by the routines that the school has developed to deal with these constraints. The bureaucratic solutions—computerized attendance records, assistant principals in charge of nonoverlapping domains, the small army of counselors with discrete responsibilities—have taken on lives of their own. In doing so, they have relieved teachers of responsibility for the students' development, diverted the attention of administrators from coherent planning, and diffused the school's sense of mission.

COMPOSITE SPECIAL-PURPOSE SCHOOL[7]

Demographics and School Site

Founded ten years ago as an educational option school, this school today serves some 1000 students from throughout New York City. (Other special-purpose schools that we studied served as many as 2600.) The student body, by city mandate, reflects both the racial and ethnic diversity of New York City's population (50 percent Hispanic, 40 percent black, 5 percent Asian, and 5 percent white) and the diversity of achievement among students in the city (25 percent below grade level, 50 percent on or near grade level, 25 percent above grade level).

Within these boundaries, however, the school had been free until three years ago to select its entering class. As a consequence, students

---

[7]This composite is drawn from the two special-purpose schools that admit a cross section of all city students. The special school for students who had been unable to cope with regular schools shares many characteristics of the schools in the composite. But because its academic and attendance standards set it apart, it is not included in the composite.

from two-parent families and students with solid attendance records in elementary or junior high school were overrepresented in the population. Many of the students whom the school previously selected came from Catholic elementary schools.

Three years ago, new city regulations required that 50 percent of entering students be selected by lottery. Since this policy was adopted, the school has inherited a number of students with historically problematic attendance records who have persisted in frequent truancy. The proportion of these students is significant enough to have affected the tone of the school as a whole.

The principal, a middle-aged white woman who is widely respected as an educational innovator, founded the school ten years ago. With a small team of trusted advisers, she sets the tone for the school, both for students and faculty. In the early years, the principal ran a summer program to orient new staff to the school's central philosophy. But the school no longer has sufficient funds for staff orientation, and socialization of new teachers is now left to department heads and other teachers.

The school is located in a large building uptown, shared with two other schools, an elementary school and a junior high. The building is clean and well maintained, and the hallways feel safe, although students report that expensive coats are stolen from lockers. Classrooms are relatively clean and decorated with the standard array of construction paper-covered bulletin boards. Space is scarce, however, and the sounds of the band practicing are likely to drift into the typing classroom, where a mathematics class is being held.

Mission

The school prepares students for nonprofessional and semiprofessional careers in health care as paramedics, laboratory technicians, dental hygienists, and nutritionists. But the serious academic content of all classes prepares students to enter four-year colleges, and most do so.

The school's principal goal is to prepare students so that they can choose between work and higher education. It teaches vocational skills but insists that students be prepared for college entry-level English, mathematics, and social science classes. Graduates are expected both to understand the working world well enough to become productive employees and good team members and to be able to think for themselves. They are taught that effective workers think and solve problems.

The school knows that many students come from homes where education is not valued for its own sake. The school views the health-care focus and attendant job prospects as a "hook" that gives the students a sense of direction and lets them justify to themselves, their parents, and their peers the effort they are putting into schoolwork. The school complements this effort by trying to create a supportive and caring environment in which each student's talents and contributions are recognized.

From the fact that students chose to enroll, the school creates a presumption that they are willing to accept the school's goals and rules. It has tried to create a tone of community and of shared enterprise instead of an emphasis on rules dictated from above. Students are asked to sign an agreement to follow the school rules that begins "I, as a member of the student body of ----- High School, am proud of my school and its image. I respect the dignity and achievements of my fellow students. I recognize the following rules and regulations which govern student behavior at my school."

Students seem to accept this framework, and older students are instrumental in acclimating younger students to the importance of subscribing to community standards. Major safety problems, such as drugs and weapons, are virtually absent from the campus. Occasional fights break out and are dealt with swiftly by immediate suspension.

The school sees itself as responsible for the development not only of a student's mind but also of his or her character. Its community service requirement (see "Curriculum," below) is one expression of this. Further manifestation comes in constant reiteration of the school's communal character and in the efforts of the faculty and the principal to serve as role models for the students.

Although the school has a typical guidance office, teachers are also expected to pay close attention to the emotional and personal needs of their students. Students having particular difficulties are assigned a faculty "buddy" who keeps track of their progress, but practical constraints (such as finding a time and private place to meet) have limited the effectiveness of this approach.

Within the school itself, the principal's presence and sense of mission provide a context in which all other discussions take place. Department heads develop curricula and make major policy decisions in light of the school's three goals. But New York city and state requirements also strongly shape the curricula, and practical concerns of space, staffing, or funding often constrain innovation.

The school has almost no parent resource base to draw on, as students come from throughout the five boroughs and convincing parents to come to school activities is almost impossible. The school sends home a newsletter to parents each semester describing the school's activities and achievements, and the principal receives many testimonials from grateful parents.

The admissions counselor must also fend off dozens of parents who would like to "pull strings" to get their children admitted. Many of these parents applied to many other magnet schools. They appear less concerned about the specifics of a school's instructional focus than about a safe, disciplined environment for their children. Most parents have low incomes, difficulties in their own lives, and a fear of authority. The principal reports little support from parents in situations in which she tries to make a case to the higher authorities.

Curriculum

The curriculum is shaped largely by a philosophy of developing both intellectual and marketable skills, specifically preparation for higher education and entry-level skills for health care. Because the school tries to squeeze so much into four years, students have few choices beyond (1) their prematriculation selection of a major course of study, (2) choice of focus in English courses in 11th and 12th grades, and (3) one or two electives during the senior year. To graduate, students must devote between seven and ten units to a structured series of courses within their major area of concentration (areas include subjects such as nutrition, dentistry, and health-care office management). In these courses, students learn such skills as typing, how to act in an office setting, and basic facts about their chosen field.

In addition to work in their major field, students must take a standard curriculum, including four years each of English and social studies and two years each of mathematics, science, and a foreign language, plus one-semester required courses in art, music, and health. About half pursue a Regents' Diploma, and those who do not are required to pass RCTs in reading, writing, and mathematics.

Social studies and "major" classes are untracked. Mathematics, English, and science each have a small honors track, medium-sized Regents' and RCT tracks, and a small "power" remedial track that seeks to mainstream students after one year. Students whose skills are only slightly below the point necessary for Regents'-level work are encouraged to enroll in special "college skills" courses in 10th and 11th grades that will enable them to take Regents' courses in the 12th.

In addition to school academic requirements, all students must participate in an off-campus internship that combines community service with an opportunity for the student to experience work in the outside world. Most students volunteer at hospitals or work for local practitioners willing to take them on in exchange for their services.

Instruction is a major focus of staff attention. Department heads work with new staff to help them understand the school's teaching philosophy. Not all teachers cooperate, and the school can do little to change those who do not teach in the preferred manner. But for the most part, the school has succeeded in creating a student-centered and nonhierarchical learning environment. According to the philosophy, students talk and think critically throughout the instructional time, and the teacher serves as a resource and a stimulus for discussion. Each student knows what the expectations for the course will be and is expected to work with the instructor to master the appropriate material. Students do a great deal of writing and independent reading, both in class and as homework, as well as a significant amount of small-group work.

Accountability

The principal has developed techniques for circumventing, to the extent possible, the constraints of the New York City public school bureaucracy. This activity occupies a significant proportion of her time and energy, but as a result of her effort, she has had the freedom to hire and retain larger numbers of good teachers who subscribe to the school's philosophy. Still, despite the principal's best efforts (e.g., "camping out at the bureau of personnel"), the school is often forced to take teachers it doesn't want, and each December, as a result of enrollment decline, it must "excess" a handful of its youngest and most enthusiastic teachers.

Staff complain about the ways that New York City regulations constrain their ability to solve problems. Although the school operates more independently than most other public schools, thanks largely to the efforts of the principal, it lacks the freedom to choose or to retain the teachers it wants. It also feels stymied by city regulations that require 50 percent of its students to be selected by lottery. Some long-time staff members fear that the school may have trouble maintaining its rigorous and focused curriculum because many of the "lottery students" resist the attendance requirements.

Despite its efforts to circumvent outside regulation wherever possible, the school must meet city and state requirements in such areas as student body diversity and selection, faculty employment and retention, curricular framework, and rules and enforcement. The principal spends a significant proportion of her time building external sources of support so that central office requirements will not dominate the school's operations. She has an important ally in the local health-care industry, which hires many of the school's graduates and is willing to put pressure on the Board of Education to sustain the program.

The principal has also worked to make the school known and admired throughout the country. By writing articles about the school's progress and encouraging visits from other educators and researchers, the principal has tried to guarantee that the school will have support to countervail any pressures from the central office. Parents are not an important source of such support. Though many parents are desperate to keep their children in the school and fear that the program might disappear, they have little capacity to protect it.

The school's warrant for bold action in building its programs comes from the success it has had in placing its graduates in jobs and colleges, its reputation as a safe and caring place, and the respect its principal has gained through her many years in the New York City schools and her contact with the health-care community.

RESULTS

By reputation, religious and special-purpose public schools experience much greater success with low-income students than do comprehensive zoned public schools. We found the reputation justified. Table 3 compares outcomes for four groups of 1990 graduating seniors in the three types of schools studied.

The zoned public schools from which our composite was drawn graduate slightly more than half of their seniors each year. Special-purpose public schools graduate about two-thirds of the entering class; Catholic schools graduate 95 percent of the class, including 82 percent of Partnership students. Only about one in 20 of the zoned schools' graduates receive the Regents' Diploma, signifying the completion of an academically demanding college preparatory program. Over half of the students in the special-purpose public schools and over two-thirds of Catholic school graduates achieve that distinction.

The proportion of graduating seniors taking the Scholastic Aptitude Test is a good proxy of the number considering reasonably selective colleges or universities. Less than one in three graduates of comprehensive high schools—presumably those most academically inclined—take the test. Fewer than one in three of these test takers place above the national average for all black students. Over 50 percent of special-purpose public school graduates take the tests, and more than 40 percent score above the black student average. The Catholic school Partnership graduates' performance is particularly noteworthy:

Table 3

COMPARATIVE SAT SCORES OF GRADUATING SENIORS IN ZONED, SPECIAL-PURPOSE, AND CATHOLIC SCHOOLS, 1990

Schools	Percentage Graduating	Percentage Taking SAT	Average Combined SAT Score	Percentage above Mean for Blacks[a]
Zoned public[b]	55	33	642	<30
Special public[b,c]	66	>50	715	>40
Catholic[d]				
Partnership students	82	85	803	>60
All students	95	85	815	>60

[a] Estimates of the proportion of students in each school scoring above the mean for black students are calculated from national SAT norms provided by the Educational Testing Service.
[b] The New York City Board of Education provided the data.
[c] The data do not include seniors in special-purpose public schools for students who had failed in zoned schools. The excluded students tend to be older and more troubled than the average zoned school students and to come from lower-income environments. They graduate at near the average rate for zoned school students, but are unlikely to aspire to a four-year college.
[d] Individual schools and the Partnership Program Office provided the data.

85 percent take the test and over 60 percent score above the average for black students.

Based on the mean scores and distributions provided by the New York City Board of Education, we calculate that only 4 percent of SAT takers in the zoned schools have scores above the national average for all students. This figure presumably includes honor students who entered the zoned schools on, or above, grade level. Over 70 percent of zoned students scored below the national average for black students.

However, score averages in all three kinds of schools studied fall below national averages for all students. But students from special-purpose public schools approach the national mean for black students, and Catholic school Partnership students comfortably exceed it. Partnership students in the Catholic schools—one-third of whom enter below grade level, many of them with freshman placement scores below the 20th percentile—scored nearly as well as their tuition-paying classmates.

These data more than prove that the three kinds of schools get different results. But the data do not answer two vital questions: (1) Are students in Catholic and special-purpose public schools so unlike those in zoned schools that valid comparisons cannot be made? (2) Do Catholic and special-purpose public schools have features that could not be reproduced in zoned public schools?

Section IV takes up these questions. We are particularly interested, with regard to the second, in understanding how schools translate broad philosophical statements of educational purpose into the habits and customs with which these schools characteristically attack instructional problems as they appear.

IV. TRANSFORMING PHILOSOPHY INTO COHERENT INSTRUCTION

How do the Catholic schools in our sample—schools that spend less money per pupil and offer far lower salaries to teachers, many of them uncertified—accomplish these results? Do they have a special supply of gifted people, or do their basic structures and incentives strengthen people of ordinary competence?

How and why do the special-purpose schools succeed? They operate, after all, in a public environment. Do they have some special cohesion that explains their effectiveness, or do they attract remarkable people? Or does even limited freedom from the constraints of bureaucratic oversight encourage extraordinary performance by typical teachers?

Finally, why are effective educators in comprehensive high schools often thought of as gifted mavericks and iconoclasts? Are the pressures to conform to routine so strong in public school systems that only extraordinary people, heroic effort, and revolutionary fervor can overcome them? Can we change the structures and incentives of public schools so that excellent performance becomes the norm?

As we observed high schools in operation, we found that different kinds of schools employ dramatically different strategies for educating disadvantaged minority children. These strategies are deeply rooted in tradition and legal requirements. Some are necessitated by funding or shortages of teachers willing to work for the wages offered.

We describe these strategies below, based on observed differences in the characteristics of whole schools, rather than differences in specific curricula, teacher traits, or student backgrounds. We show the importance of a clearly defined sense of school purpose combined with the organizational cohesion and flexibility to pursue that purpose, however defined. In these two characteristics, in particular, we found Catholic and special-purpose public schools to be remarkably alike, and together they differed substantially from zoned public schools.

FOCUS SCHOOLS CONCEPT

We use the word *focus* to describe the characteristics that Catholic and special-purpose public schools appear to have in common. Focus schools resemble one another in three basic ways:

- Focus schools are free of external and internal barriers to invention and initiative. The concept is broad, but it is not all-inclusive. In fact, it almost certainly excludes most of the public schools in the United States.
- Focus schools have clear, uncomplicated missions centered on the experiences the school intends to provide its students and on the ways the students will benefit and change in response to those experiences.
- Focus schools are strong organizations with a capacity to initiate action in pursuit of their missions, to sustain themselves over time, and to manage their external relationships.

Zoned public schools, in contrast, have diffuse missions defined by the diverse demands of external funders and regulators. They are also profoundly compromised as organizations, with little capacity to initiate their own solutions to problems, define their own internal character, or manage their relationships with external audiences.

The constraints on zoned schools, and the habits people in them have adopted in response to those constraints, hinder effective operation. These schools show the effects of a long succession of choices and compromises, none of which was intended to produce the kinds of schools now typical of inner cities. As a result, people in zoned schools—teachers, administrators, and even students—do not operate as effectively as they might.

The broad categories of mission and organizational strength, noted above, include several more specific features that both distinguish focus schools from zoned comprehensive schools and explain the focus schools' particular strengths in educating disadvantaged minority students. The missions of focus and zoned public schools differ in the following ways:

- Focus schools concentrate on student outcomes to the virtual exclusion of all other matters. Zoned schools focus primarily on delivering programs and following procedures.
- Focus schools have strong social contracts that communicate the reciprocal responsibilities of administration, students, and teachers and establish the benefits that each can derive from fulfilling the contract faithfully. Zoned schools try whenever possible to let staff and students define their own roles in the school.
- Focus schools have a strong commitment to parenting, acting aggressively to mold student attitudes and values. Zoned schools see themselves primarily as transmitters of information and imparters of skills.

- Focus schools have centripetal curricula that draw all students toward learning certain core skills and perspectives. Zoned schools distinguish sharply among students in terms of ability and preference and offer profoundly different curricula to different groups.

With regard to organization, focus and zoned schools differ as follows:

- Focus schools operate as problem-solving organizations, taking the initiative to change their programs in response to emerging needs. External mandates and rigid internal divisions of labor constrain the problem-solving capabilities of zoned schools.
- Focus schools sustain their own organizational character, both by attracting staff members who accept the school's premises and by socializing new staff members. Zoned schools have little capacity to select staff or influence the attitudes or behavior of new staff members.
- Focus schools consider themselves accountable to the people who depend on their performance—parents, students, neighborhood and parish groups, financial supporters, and admirers elsewhere in the community. Zoned schools answer primarily to bureaucratic superiors, including outside rule-making, auditing, and assessment organizations.

In short, focus schools are designed to influence and change students. Zoned schools are designed to administer programs and deliver services.

MISSION

A school's mission affects all aspects of its life, from formal activities, such as instruction and student assessment, to informal interactions between students, teachers, and administrators. Activities that contribute to the school's mission get a great deal of attention, and other activities are, perforce, relatively neglected. Missions are the premises from which priorities are set and problems are solved. The staff and students of focus schools—both religious and special purpose—clearly understand their schools' mission.[1]

---

[1] In our student survey, focus school students were significantly more likely than zoned school students to agree with the statement, "You get the sense that everyone in this school is working towards the same goal." See survey results in the appendix.

Concentration on Student Outcomes

Although defining desired outcomes does not guarantee attaining them, the schools in our study proved remarkably capable at doing what they set out to do. As a key mission, the focus schools sought from the beginning to serve a cross section of disadvantaged city students. With that goal uppermost, administrators and teachers keenly observed and critiqued their own efforts and willingly changed programs that did not appear to work. Staff were committed to the job and thought of themselves as the people best qualified to do it. They did not criticize or become disillusioned with students when educational efforts proved unsuccessful.

Missions of Focus Schools. Concern for student outcomes, particularly the introduction of moral and religious values and preparation for expected roles in society, drives Catholic schools' missions. The inner-city Catholic high schools resemble the more elite preparatory schools run by religious orders in their concern for moral values, but they differ in their expectations for a student's ultimate role in society. The elite Catholic schools expect their graduates to become leaders in professions, business, politics, and the church. The inner-city schools expect their students to be productive upstanding citizens but not necessarily community or intellectual leaders.

The missions of special-purpose public schools also center on the student, but they focus more on the delivery of a particular curriculum than do the Catholic schools. In many cases, the special-purpose schools have ambitious aspirations for students—they hope to prepare students for admission to four-year colleges, business careers, or highly skilled trades—but the aspirations are generally less specific about the nature of graduates' future lives. In our sample, and more generally in New York City and across the country, a few special-purpose public schools have very definite expectations, especially for their disadvantaged and minority students, i.e., that they will become effective leaders on behalf of their groups. These schools deliberately politicize their students, urging them, as do some elite Catholic schools, to prepare for lives of activism and political involvement.

Missions of Zoned Schools. Administrators in some of the zoned schools that we studied were able to locate the formal mission statements adopted when the schools were first opened. The original missions resembled those of elite preparatory schools: preparation for higher education and civic leadership. But those statements were, in the eyes of administration and faculty, written for another time and are largely unrealistic now. Schools could seek such goals for the first- and second-generation European immigrant children for whom they were first built. But for the low-income African American and Hispanic immigrant children that the schools serve today, such aspirations, in the eyes of school staff, are unrealistic.

The schools' present-day realistic aspirations are to (1) manage the array of instructional and social service programs available for their students, (2) keep as many students as possible in school long enough to enable them to leave with some credential (a diploma or some certificate of completion), and (3) provide students with at least some of the skills required for entry into the labor market.

Zoned schools, in short, are formal institutions administering programs of benefits and entitlements, while focus schools are informal, self-contained institutions applying general values and priorities in the service of students. Zoned schools have many competing philosophies, rather than one clear overarching one. Catholic and special-purpose public schools have clear and definite philosophies, but enjoy great flexibility in deciding how to apply those philosophies to particular students. In the absence of a clear central mission or philosophy, zoned schools are controlled essentially by piecemeal demands, rules, claimed entitlements, and contractual provisions.

Many staff members in zoned schools attach their careers to some externally mandated activity; within the school, issues not controlled by specific external requirements are decided through negotiation among contending groups, each of which has some claim founded in law, contract, regulation, or the traditional way of doing things. Everyone in the school—student, faculty, and administration—sees the school's mission from a perspective defined by his or her responsibilities or group affiliations. Students are seen in terms of the attributes that determine their eligibility for particular programs.

The fractionization of zoned schools means that no one is responsible for the student as a whole person or for integrating the school's many educational programs. As the vice principal at one zoned school said, "This school is too complex for anyone to understand."

Social Contract

The school's mission is more than a simple statement of intent or a broadly shared agreement about the preferred tone of student-teacher relations. It is, in effect, a contract about how the administration, faculty, and students will behave so as to achieve the school's goals and preserve its desired climate. It is a bargain that the school offers students and staff members, and that they tacitly accept by joining the school community.

All the schools that we studied, including the zoned schools, had some form of social contract. But the contracts varied profoundly on what was expected of the administration, faculty, and students, and how the system of reciprocal obligations was to be enforced.

Social Contracts in Focus Schools. The typical social contract that a focus school offers a student may be summarized as follows:

> We have something valuable to give you. We'll work hard to enable you to get it, but you have to meet us at least part way. That means accepting our basic goals and standards and making a real effort on your schoolwork. If you do that, we will treat you with respect. If you do not initially accept our goals and standards, we will help you to understand why they are valuable, but if you are stubborn, you must leave. Though your future job and academic opportunities depend on how hard you try and how well you do here, we can and will work to give you the best feasible opportunity for a good job or college placement.[2]

Focus schools explain the preexisting contract to students when they enroll. The faculty and staff take pains to inform students about the terms of the bargain and to persuade skeptical newcomers of its value. Catholic schools in particular aggressively indoctrinate new students and staff to their norms and expectations. Some create big-brother and big-sister programs with older students serving as models and guides. They do not assume that students will automatically fit in, but they do assume that the school can change students' attitudes and behavior.

Though students and staff get help learning and adjusting to the social contract, the schools do not offer to renegotiate its basic terms. Focus schools are not democracies. They are, in the terms introduced by Peters and Waterman, tight-loose organizations.[3] They require tight adherence to missions and principles, but are loose in allowing great latitude in how the mission and principles are to be advanced. Thus, members of the organization are willing members of the social contract, even if they did not formulate it in the first place.

---

[2]The social contract in the school designed for students who had been unable to adjust to regular schools could be expressed as follows: You are in serious trouble. We're here to help you and we can help you. We understand the difficulties that brought you here, but we won't lie to you about the fact that you are in trouble and have a long way to go. But if you can just stick with us and make some effort, we will give you as much education as you can handle. The result may not be a ticket to college or a professional job, but what you learn here can make you a productive adult and may save your life.

[3]See Thomas J. Peters and Robert H. Waterman, *In Search of Excellence*, Harper and Row, New York, 1982.

Most students flout the contract at some time, but they find the consequences adverse, swift, and sure. Students or staff who cannot tolerate the contract are free to leave. Because the contract offers the students significant benefits, and because few people enter the school without some understanding of its basic terms, few choose to leave.

Social Contracts in Zoned Schools. The typical social contract in a zoned school can be summarized as follows:

> We are obligated to run this school and you are obligated to be here. While you are here, we hope that you will take advantage of what we make available. If we can help remove obstacles to your taking advantage of the programs here, we will do so. We will ensure that you are safe while you are here. If you ask us for specific help, we will almost surely give it. If you do not call attention to your needs, we probably will not notice the problem. We can't do much to control your behavior, but if your attendance here makes life unbearable for others, we would prefer that you leave.

The vagueness of the zoned schools' mission extends to the social contract. Beyond ensuring students' safety, the schools guarantee only to offer instruction. Zoned schools follow the university model, promoting compartmentalization of students' and faculty members' time along lines of academic specialties. Teachers are primarily purveyors of specialized bodies of knowledge; they can decide to deal with students on a wider basis—e.g., integrating disciplines or considering the student's broader development—but they are under no particular pressure to do so.

The weak social contract in zoned schools is intended to defer to students' wishes. But our interviews revealed that students resented the zoned schools' diffidence. Students in all the zoned schools that we studied complained about teachers who made such statements as "I get paid whether you learn or not." Similarly, students in all zoned schools resented teachers who did not demand respect and permitted students to disrupt classes. As one student said, "The thing I hate is when the teachers let boys curse them. If they won't stand up for themselves, they won't help you."

Consequences of Different Social Contracts. The contrast is most vivid between zoned and Catholic school contracts: Students in Catholic schools said that teachers demonstrate their commitment by saying, "I can stay here until you learn this. I'm already home; I live upstairs." Priests and nuns who live in the school building are obviously uniquely equipped to make such a statement.

But the underlying message—that learning is a cooperative enterprise and the teacher feels obligated to do more than simply present material—can be sent in other ways. In special-purpose public schools, a similar message is typically sent by the teacher's departure from prepared lesson plans, a departure that approaches a problem from a new angle and requires extra effort on both the student's and teacher's part.

Though the social contract usually focuses on learning, it can have implications for how the school will deal with the nonacademic sides of student life. A school that expects little of its students has a weak warrant for controlling behavior.[4] All schools must exert some control over students, at a minimum to guarantee physical safety, but schools without strong social contracts must rely on specific do's and don'ts.

Zoned schools have rules, but they are highly specific and rely on the authority of the school administration rather than on broad principles derived from joint goals and reciprocal obligations. When such narrowly drawn rules are violated, teachers and administrators face a dilemma: They must either apply the rules strictly in every case, or risk discrediting the rules through lenient application. Few choose the former approach, because it requires harsh action against children whose lives are already too difficult. Understandably, most opt for leniency. Teachers who believe that an incident requires firm application of the rules must act on their own initiative, in virtual isolation from broader institutional support.

When discipline is based on an explicit agreement about the school's mission and all parties' reciprocal obligations, teachers and administrators can afford to forgive repentant violators and withhold punishment because leniency does not weaken the contractual base on which rules are founded. Standards rooted in the school's social contract also perform the vital function of teaching students how to live in an organization and respond to legitimate expectations about reliability, reciprocity, and respect for others' rights.

When disciplinary standards are not linked to a mutually beneficial contract, students learn that the rules are arbitrary and unrelated to their own interests. Because the rules are integral to the life of the school, issues of crime and punishment receive relatively little attention in focus schools. In the zoned schools, however, issues of deportment, attitude, and discipline consume much of the time of teachers and administrators.

The social contract includes consistent student attendance in focus schools; in zoned schools it does not.[5] As zoned school administrators

---

[4]In our student survey, students in focus schools were significantly more likely than students in zoned schools to say that students act respectfully toward the school, teachers, and one another, and to say that students take the rules seriously; see the appendix.

[5]In the student survey, focus school students were significantly more likely than zoned school students to say, "Attendance is good here: students come to school and go to class." See the appendix.

told us, poor attendance is not limited to a few habitual truants. All students, even those who are relatively serious about their studies, miss several days a month. Students assume that the school will make allowances for their absence. One student who was unable to answer a question in class said, "You can't expect me to know that. I wasn't here when you taught it. If I had been here, I would have known."

Zoned school students know that a good part of the student body—on some days nearly half—is at large in the neighborhood. Thus, students need not feel isolated from the school community if they are absent. The companionship of other students who are absent from school is an attractive alternative to school attendance. Because the school does not treat absence as a violation of the social contract, students can choose absence on a given day without fear of punishment or isolation from peers. By contrast, focus students isolate themselves from the school community by staying home, and they face academic and social penalties when they return to school.

In all the schools that we visited, students would tell teachers if someone had brought a gun into school or intended to do physical harm to a classmate. But students in Catholic and special-purpose public schools would normally tell teachers why another student was missing from class; students in zoned public schools normally would not.

Commitment to Parenting

All the schools that we studied respected their students' growing powers and aspirations. But focus schools acted as parents, trying to mold students' values and channel their behavior. Zoned schools treated students as adults whose basic values and preferences were already formed and must be treated with deference.

Parenting in Focus Schools. Focus schools address the parenting role directly. Catholic schools have a commitment to guide and mold the children in their care, and staff members believe that aggressive socialization is warranted both by the inherent validity of the school's premises and by the implied consent of parents and children. Special-purpose public schools feel free to hold children to the standards required by the school's own philosophy. This attribute not only preserves the school but also fulfills the fundamental commitment that special-purpose schools share with Catholic schools: to teach students that actions have consequences.

In general, focus schools accept responsibility for teaching children that personal responsibility, reciprocity, reliability, and thoughtfulness are indispensable traits of a competent adult. They also teach that coercion, deception, and intimidation are unacceptable and dangerous in any context. They teach these lessons by providing students the experience of living within an adult-style social contract.

The school for students who had failed elsewhere also held a daily "family group," in which students discussed social issues and their own problems in developing the discipline necessary to finish school. The group leaders (who were teachers in the school's academic programs) stressed the importance of learning to understand the broader society and rejecting the role of "a victim of uncontrollable forces."

Some focus schools teach classes in ethics or moral values. But their basic strategy for socializing students is to make the school's internal transactions a learning experience. As one Catholic school principal said, "We have to give them good models of adult behavior and expect them to follow [the models] at all times. If we shout at them, they will shout at us. . . . One thing we will never tolerate is for one student to hit or intimidate another. We teach that you cannot harm another human being."

Parenting in Zoned Schools. Zoned public schools do not aspire to as strong a socializing role as do focus schools. Rather, they take deference to the student's own values as a defining characteristic. Some teach classes in religious systems or values and provide individual counseling for troubled students.

In their daily operations, however, zoned schools do not act as if they have a responsibility to show students that actions have consequences. Indeed, in the hope of encouraging students, they give them passing grades for substandard work or water down the content of science and mathematics courses. Likewise, zoned schools often tolerate disruptive behavior, both because they fear a more assertive response would depress student attendance and because the necessary actions stress teachers.

Focus school staffs believe that a policy of shielding children from the consequences of their actions deprives them of important lessons about the adult world, e.g., that performance is often measured by absolute, not relative, standards and that serious enterprises cannot tolerate disruptive behavior.

Staffs of zoned schools, in contrast, act as if they cannot hold their students to the prevailing societal standards of behavior and academic performance. By adopting lower standards, zoned schools exacerbate their students' deprivation. In truth, zoned schools are not indifferent: Their administrators and faculty often care deeply about the children and their emotional well-being. But they are diffident, that is, unwilling to impose standards and make judgments.

Zoned schools base concern for students' emotional lives on self-esteem, i.e., acceptance of the positive aspects of one's social or ethnic identity. Well-motivated though that effort may be, it differs fundamentally from the focus school efforts to change and mold the student.

Even if they wanted to play a more aggressive parenting role, zoned schools would be handicapped by the transience of staff members and the practice of changing class registrations every semester. Most students stay with a teacher for only one semester before moving to another one-semester course. Teachers say that they barely have time to learn their students' names before a course is finished. Furthermore, some departments lose as many as one in five teachers during the midyear citywide staff cuts. The brevity and instability of student-teacher contact hinders the formation of personal relationships.

Centripetal Curriculum

Consistent with their simple missions, focus schools try to expose all students to coursework that imparts the basic linguistic, historical, and mathematical understandings that have traditionally been the goals of high school education. In contrast, zoned schools provide varied curricula, some of which do not cover the traditional high school material.

Tracking in Focus Schools. The programs of focus schools reflect efforts to help poorly prepared students. Though success rates vary, the schools' basic strategy is to assimilate all students into the main curriculum as quickly as possible. They assign some students to catch-up classes but regard remediation as a temporary expedient.

Focus schools unhesitatingly place burdens on their low-achieving students. Students requiring remedial help are expected to put in extra hours before and after school. Catholic school students who have not made up most of the necessary ground are expected to attend summer school. After ninth grade (tenth in the most extreme cases) they are pulled into the regular curriculum. Some continue to receive personalized help and go into classes that cover the regular curriculum material, but more slowly and at less depth.

Everyone learns from high school-level texts; no one spends class time doing basic skill drills in workbooks. In tenth grade, for example, all students read and discuss a Shakespeare play. But the slower classes spend more time on vocabulary and discussions of plot than do the faster classes, which concentrate on historical context and analysis of literary references. Students in slower English classes are also assigned to heterogeneous groups for social studies, history, and in the case of Catholic schools, religion.

All students are exposed to the basic science, mathematics, literature, and history that the school considers essential knowledge for a high school graduate. Exposure to the more challenging material, and to the performance levels of abler students, is thought to improve the performance of low-achieving students.[6] Even the vocationally oriented special-purpose schools in our sample took care to expose all students to the basic high school academic material in the course of their specified programs for different kinds of career placement.

Tracking in Zoned Schools. The comprehensive zoned school assigns students to different instructional programs on the basis of their academic development, mastery of English, and attitudes about schooling. Though some students switch from one instructional program to another, many spend their entire high school careers in the program to which they were assigned in ninth grade. Students in remedial and special education programs are particularly likely to remain in lower tracks and unlikely to gain any exposure to standard courses in algebra, literature, and science.

Several factors determine zoned schools' approach to the education of the lowest achieving. First, and most important in the minds of people who run zoned schools, is the relatively high concentration of students with very poor academic skills. Such students also attend focus schools, but in smaller numbers. Large numbers of such students enable zoned schools to offer entire instructional programs for them.

The availability of special programs can itself create labeling. Ten years ago, a RAND study showed that the use of the "learning disability" label varied from one school to another, depending on administrators' habits and availability of programs.[7] In the New York City zoned schools, special education labels are used freely, especially for black male students. In the zoned schools that we visited, over 25 percent of black male students, compared to 12 percent of the overall student body, entered special education programs.

Some students in zoned schools may indeed have more profound academic or emotional problems than any in focus schools. But the latter schools are also much more reluctant to designate students as handicapped. Catholic schools do not admit students with profound cognitive handicaps, but some students who fit the public schools'

---

[6]In our student survey, focus school students were significantly more likely than zoned school students to say that students believe that it is good to do well in school and work hard at schoolwork, and to disagree with the statements, "Students here are happy just to pass; they don't worry about doing well," and "Teachers here are satisfied as long as you pass; they don't care so much about your really learning or doing well." See the appendix.

[7]Jackie Kimbrough and Paul T. Hill, *The Aggregate Effects of Federal Education Programs*, The RAND Corporation, Santa Monica, Calif., R-2638-ED, September 1981.

definition of learning disabled are admitted and served in the regular program with supplementary tutoring. In focus schools, students are presumed to fit into the main curriculum until they manifestly and repeatedly fail in it. This practice contrasts sharply with that of zoned schools, which sort students into special curricula based on tests administered on admission.

The zoned schools' eagerness to categorize students reflects their general approach, i.e., to engage students' interest in any way possible and to proliferate programs for identifiable groups. Zoned schools administer programs, and some principals take pride in the proliferation and diversity of their programs.

In one interview, a zoned school principal spent 30 minutes describing the special programs, ranging from special attendance incentives to day care for students' children, available in the school. That school's core strategy, according to the principal, is "to meet everyone's need with a program." Once a need is identified, it must have a program with an identifiable funding source, specialized staff, and reporting relationships to program monitors outside the school. The school provides classroom space and basic support. The principal and other senior administrators see as their fundamental role the fair allocation of resources among claimants and the arbitration of disputes.

Student bodies as diverse as those served by zoned schools are hard to integrate. But there is no doubt that the zoned schools solidify the distinctions that exist and create others. Zoned schools provide special programs for motivated and able students and for students with easily categorized pathologies or problems. They also group students of apparently average ability. Separation from higher-achieving students means that many average students in zoned schools lack perspective on their own performance levels.

Low standards even in honors programs deprive capable students of appropriate standards by which to judge their own achievements. Typical of the abler students that we interviewed was one bright and aggressive young woman who was maintaining a modest grade point average in a watered-down curriculum that gave her only a cursory exposure to second-year algebra and quantitative chemistry and physics. She said, "I was afraid you couldn't learn at this school, but I have done fine. I think I can go to SUNY [State University of New York] and do well enough in sciences to become an obstetrician."[8]

---

[8]See Imani Perry, "A Black Student's Reflection on Public and Private Schools," *Harvard Educational Review*, Vol. 58, No. 3, August 1988, pp. 332–336, for one student's comparison of academic standards at zoned and private high schools.

ORGANIZATIONAL STRENGTH

Initiative in Problem Solving

A school's problem-solving capacity involves two factors: an organizational habit of taking the initiative and flexible resources that can be redeployed when new problems arise.

Problem Solving in Focus Schools. Although basic principles guide the educational process in focus schools, the process is constantly being revised in response to student needs. The schools are structured to solve problems. Administrators evaluate curricula and pedagogy, but they do not try to control the academic program in detail. They control the premises under which teachers and others work—the school's mission and the priorities derived from it—not the details of pedagogy.

Problems are not always easily or successfully solved; most of the focus schools that we studied find that their jobs are growing harder as their students' families and other social supports weaken. But such schools are inherently more flexible and adept at problem solving than are the zoned public schools.

Many special-purpose public schools exist because of the initiative and entrepreneurship of their administrators and staff. The habit of initiative is part of their basic identity. Administrators and staff have created the school by seizing control of resources, creating an overarching mission that weakens the influence of external regulations, and hiring others whose commitment to the school's mission at least partly countervails other loyalties (e.g., to the union contract or to a teacher's academic discipline).

Catholic schools have a high capacity for problem solving because, among other reasons, they have lower internal transaction costs thanks to the fact that their tradition is well understood. As a result, the people involved can anticipate and understand one another's behavior relatively easily. The schools' guiding principles have worked well for a long time. Competent people can use the principles to solve problems.

Problem Solving in Zoned Schools. Zoned public schools are potentially better equipped than Catholic schools to solve new problems, because they have larger and more diverse staffs and can deliver a much wider array of services. Moreover, they have many competent and committed teachers and administrators who reach out to students and make extra efforts at their own initiative. However, the schools are so constrained by their bureaucratic organization, and by their obligations to external funding sources and regulations for almost every program, that they can do little to adapt.

Consistent with their general emphasis on a program for every problem, zoned schools discourage individual initiative in problem solving by emphasizing formal systems over personal judgment. The point is best illustrated from our field notes on three zoned schools:

> The school has a computerized entry system. In the morning, each student presents a computer-coded badge. The computer produces daily attendance reports automatically. A complementary computerized system identifies students who are in the school but cut particular classes. Each teacher's class attendance log is entered every day and matched to the school entry log. Students who habitually cut classes are identified, and the teacher whose classes are cut gets a notice to inquire. But by the time teachers inquire, many students have fallen behind and become habitual absentees.
>
> During my interview with the attendance coordinator I noticed that the street outside was full of students at 1:30. When I asked whether those students were on an early release schedule, I was told, "No, they are cutting. Sometimes there are more of them out there, and they pull up cars and play the radios on top volume. Then we have to call the police to disperse them." In answer to my question, "Does anybody ever go out and shoo them back into the school?" he responded, "No, then they would just be in the halls."
>
> I saw the attendance operation. It is a large boiler room with six extremely earnest and efficient staff members. They keep a log on each student's attendance, call parents of each student who has more than five absences in a month, initiate home visits, and refer hard cases to the Board's truant officers. The tracking system is apparently very efficient; workers were able to retrieve an attendance summary on any student in about two minutes. Staff complained that few of the frequent absentees had stable addresses and telephone numbers. According to the director, the staff "can't find any point of contact for many of these students. The truant officers are totally overwhelmed by the caseload. . . . I send them paper and they send me paper. Nothing much can be done."

In all these instances, the people in the school had created a technically sophisticated and well-designed system to solve a problem. The system, however, had come to substitute for human judgment rather than to supplement it. Staff members' responsibility was defined in terms of operating the system and responding to its cues. If the system did not solve the problem, or if student behavior changed so that the system no longer addressed the problem, no one was responsible.

Aggressive Socialization of Teachers

The strength of a school organization depends on the extent to which it can manage and influence its staff members. The teaching and administrative staff represent the school's capital. Without the capacity to select staff members whose abilities and attitudes match the school's mission, no school can remain a strong organization.

All public schools draw staff members from the same pool of certified teachers maintained by the Board of Education. Catholic schools draw from a somewhat broader pool, including both certified and noncertified teachers.

The focus schools have the advantage of clearly defined identities that attract some teachers and, presumably, discourage others. The zoned schools have the disadvantage of negative reputations based on publicity about violence, poor attendance, and high dropout rates.[9]

But none of the schools has the capacity to handpick teachers to fit needs precisely. Most teachers in all three types of schools arrive as little-known quantities. The differences between focus and zoned schools are evident in their efforts to influence teachers' performance once they are hired.

Staff Socialization in Focus Schools. By defining the reciprocal responsibilities of teachers, students, and administrators, a focus school's social contract provides the framework for influencing teacher attitudes and performance. Staff members depend on one another to do their jobs. They openly discuss the problems and needs of students whom they teach in common; teachers do not hesitate to discuss the inadequacies of their older students' preparation in early years.[10]

Teachers' strengths and weaknesses in dealing with students are widely known. No school has a fast-acting or foolproof method for improving individual teacher performance. But administrators in focus

---

[9]Principals in the various schools used very different criteria to screen potential teachers. Special-purpose public schools emphasized compatibility with the school's own academic focus and collaborative working style. Catholic schools emphasized a liking for the teaching process itself; if faced with a choice between a subject-matter expert without teaching experience and a teacher who had proved himself or herself in elementary school, many Catholic school principals would choose the latter. Principals in zoned public schools wanted teachers who were competent instructors and knowledgeable subject-matter specialists, but they agreed that ability to control a class and avoid needless confrontations with students was the irreducible minimum qualification.

[10]See Rosenholtz's description of teacher interactions in schools where teachers share a sense of mission. Her contrasting description of teacher peer interactions in schools where teachers regard themselves as isolated solo practitioners is vivid: "[T]he substance of their conversations rarely includes instructional topics to avoid any conclusions about the relative competence implied by requesting or offering assistance.... [Many conversations emphasize] besting behavior, the way in which teachers handled student discipline problems, demeaning remarks about students' lack of academic success.... The significance of nonproductive conversational exchange ... may be its reinforcement of disengaged teacher behavior and its legitimation of ineffective—if not outright deleterious—work with students." Susan J. Rosenholtz, "Effective Schools: Interpreting the Evidence," *American Journal of Education*, Vol. 93, No. 3, May 1985, pp. 363–366.

schools take responsibility for compensating students for teachers' weaknesses. The principal of one Catholic school told us:

> We know who the weak teachers are. But we make sure that no student gets two straight years of weak teachers. If we must assign a class to a poorer teacher, we make sure the students get one of the best teachers the next year and that teacher knows they need some help getting up to speed.

Catholic schools regard teacher improvement as an internal problem: Poor performers are counseled, observed, and advised by department heads and senior administrators. Catholic schools can seldom afford vendor-provided staff development or training courses. Some teachers are ultimately advised to leave, but most, with help, are able to meet the school's standards. Special-purpose public schools (like zoned schools and unlike Catholic schools) are often able to obtain supplementary training for teachers.

The staff members of focus schools are also socialized to their responsibilities to one another. The basic organization of these schools accentuates interdependency. For financial reasons, Catholic schools use substitute teachers sparingly, so teachers must fill in for one another during brief illnesses and emergency absences. Because teachers who are absent impose burdens on their colleagues, teacher absences are rare.

Staff Socialization in Zoned Schools. Zoned public schools are organized to let teachers operate as autonomously as possible. Teachers are responsible for their own classes, but issues of overall student development are usually left to the counseling department. An elaborate systemwide process for finding and paying substitutes insulates teachers from the consequences of one another's absences, with the predictable consequence that teacher absenteeism is much higher in zoned than in focus schools.

To improve teacher performance, zoned schools rely on formal staff development courses. Teachers with inadequate skills or problems in relating to students are sent outside the school for specific training. Though some teachers and department heads offer help and advice, teacher improvement is basically an external process. Teachers who cannot or will not improve are written off as hopeless cases but are tolerated because of the high bureaucratic cost of termination.

Accountability

All schools answer to outside authorities. But focus and zoned schools answer to different authorities and for different purposes.

Accountability in Focus Schools. Faculty and staff of focus schools are accountable to one another and to the school's immediate community—parents, students, and others who depend on their performance. Higher authorities exist, but they do not figure prominently in the school's day-to-day operation.

Catholic schools nominally belong to a hierarchical organization, with the central Catholic schools office, the head of the religious order that staffs the school, and the local pastor all technically superior to the principal. But these entities are in no position to observe performance in detail or to control day-to-day activities. The New York City central Catholic schools office, for example, manages the 12th largest school system in the United States with fewer than 30 employees.

External authorities can intervene forcefully when a Catholic school's failures become conspicuous. But in most matters and at most times, Catholic schools are, in effect, accountable to the values embodied in the staff, the parents, and students who use the schools, and to alumni groups and other direct financial supporters.

Special-purpose public schools ultimately depend on the New York City Board of Education for financial allocations and for teacher assignments, and they must file the same information as zoned public schools on such matters as finances, student attendance, and student test scores. But most special-purpose schools have external constituencies that balance central office pressures.

Many special-purpose schools with career or vocational foci enjoy the support of employers and postsecondary institutions that take their graduates. Schools with charismatic principals often gain citywide—in some cases nationwide—attention, and their admirers and imitators also help reduce the schools' vulnerability to the central office. Some principals transform the regulatory pressures that debilitate zoned schools into assets, rallying internal support against threats from the outside.

The fact that both students and faculty are in focus schools by choice profoundly affects accountability in these schools. Because many advocate consumer choice as the keystone of educational reform, we looked closely at how it affected the operation of these schools. Clearly, consumer influence is a factor in these schools, but the choice relationships we saw were richer and more complex and reciprocal than we expected.

In the focus schools that we studied, parents do not control the school, and their concerns do not overtly influence day-to-day decisionmaking. Nor, in fact, are parents involved to any great extent in decisionmaking, administration, instruction, or noninstructional support. Parents support the school by choosing it for their children and ensuring student attendance, but they are not partners in the educational process. School staff respect parents' ultimate authority over their children but do not defer to parents on educational matters.

In focus schools, accountability runs in several directions. Students are responsible to their parents and to faculty for their own effort and performance. The school is responsible to parents, but parents understand that the school operates through the intense personal effort of the principal and other key staff members. The unending financial problems of most (and the recent closure of some) inner-city parochial schools and the constant threat that new central office regulations will cripple special-purpose public schools underscore the schools' vulnerability. Parents' fear that the school will disappear is as strong and well founded as administrators' fear that parents will take their children out of the school.

Chosen schools run on more than consumer sovereignty. Staff, parents, and students have reasons to see themselves as joined in a common enterprise. As a consequence, focus schools work hard to help and keep students and teachers who are not making the grade. Despite the popular conception, Catholic schools do not maintain their standards by expelling large numbers of students. Once students are admitted or teachers are hired, the schools' leaders feel committed to the individuals and want them to succeed. Despite their reluctance to expel or fire, however, the principal and staff have real leverage if they decide a student's or teacher's behavior must be changed.

Parents know what the school offers and trust it to operate effectively in their child's interest. All parties know the principles that underlie the children's education, if not exactly how each child will be handled. We encountered Catholic school students who are the latest of many family members to attend the same school. As school administrators explain, the families know that children have different needs and do not expect the school to treat all identically. But they do trust the school to make sympathetic and competent judgments in each child's case. Trust and loyalty, not consumer fickleness, mark such parent-school relationships.

Accountability in Zoned Schools. Zoned schools, in contrast, have almost entirely hierarchical accountability relationships. Because the schools lack both particular identities and close connections with external forces that admire them or rely on their performance, administrators' careers depend on the approval of the Board of Education and its central administrative staff of 4800.[11] Likewise, teachers' promotion and transfer opportunities depend largely on the central

---

[11] This number excludes the administrative staffs of the 32 community districts.

personnel office and the union. These schools also count heavily on categorical programs that provide special funds and staff to serve particular disadvantaged student groups.

All these external authorities mandate the use of standard performance measuring systems; the overriding goal of school staff is to perform well on these measurements. Such measures are intended to reflect the quality of the school's service to students. However, most of them are imposed and evaluated piecemeal.

Zoned schools report student attendance figures to one external organization, achievement test scores to a second, student health measures to a third. School staff try to produce good scores on all the measures, but their relative emphasis changes from time to time, as the vigilance of different outside authorities varies. When we visited the zoned schools, student attendance rates were prominently discussed in the newspapers and by the school board, and schools were accordingly doing everything they could to stimulate attendance. In some schools this emphasis discouraged faculty from confronting students lounging in the halls or disrupting classes for fear the students would stop coming to school at all.

Because virtually everyone in zoned schools is assigned there by external authorities, staff members have little sense of a personal contract with students, parents, or one another. Most are committed professionals, but they are attached more to abstract principles than to individuals.

Zoned schools are more likely to accept a student's or teacher's poor performance as a given and to work around problem cases, assigning bad teachers to low-priority classes and tolerating student absenteeism. For zoned-school professionals, accountability means doing as well as possible on the statistics kept by the central office. It does not mean reaching and implementing a contract with individual students, teachers, or families.

CONCLUSIONS

Everything about a focus school—its mission, internal structure, staff incentives, and external relationships—is concentrated on educating and influencing students. It candidly explains to students their needs for further intellectual and character development. It puts students under strong pressure to learn, to behave in constructive ways, and to develop adult attitudes about personal responsibility. Finally, it is organized to resist external pressures that would deflect staff and student attention from the missions of instruction and socialization.

We formulated the concept of focus schools to encompass the strong similarities that we saw between Catholic and special-purpose public schools. We were not the first, however, to recognize the desirability of these schools' attributes. Many reformers have urged public school systems to change their comprehensive schools in ways that would endow them with the characteristics of the focus schools.[12]

The most important similarity between the focus school concept and reformers' recommendations involves the concern for the school as a functioning, self-sustaining, problem-solving organization. This concern constitutes the central message of the literature on effective schools inspired by Ronald Edmonds and developed by Brookover, Lezotte, and others.[13] Shanker has also written about the need to strengthen schools' internal incentive systems and to create teacher-student bonds that will enable the school to influence students' lives.[14] The reforms advocated by Sizer, Goodlad, and Comer all emphasize the importance of making the school a community with strong internal bonds and a capacity for guiding its members.[15]

The movement for site-based management also focuses reform efforts on the individual school, rather than on district or statewide policies, mandates, targets, incentive schemes, or standardized

---

[12] As early as 1981, Tomlinson argued that "certain characteristics of pre-1950s schooling ... are inherently necessary for learning, regardless of a child's ability or background.... These necessary conditions include teachers willing and able to teach, a curriculum that everyone can learn, order and stability in the learning environment, minimal distraction from the learning process, and children willing and able to learn what they are taught. The delicacies of fashion notwithstanding, all of these conditions must obtain at once to establish an effective learning context. When the conditions are optimal, achievement theoretically is limited only by individual differences in the abilities and effort of the children and the teachers. Put differently, under optimal conditions the structure and events that surround and make up the classroom do not distract from learning, and children's and the teacher's own resources, their abilities and efforts, can, for better or worse, be fully expressed. When one or more of these conditions is sub-optimal, achievement will be reduced. To illustrate: We have spent considerable time and money on improving the quality of teaching and curricula, and—in the lab—the improvements have worked reasonably well. The effect of these efforts, however, has been lost when placed in a context of instability and distraction, a state characterizing many schools, most visibly those in the inner city." See Tommy M. Tomlinson, "The Troubled Years: An Interpretive Analysis of Public Schools Since 1950," *Phi Delta Kappan*, Vol. 62, No. 5, January 1981, pp. 371–377.

[13] See Ronald R. Edmonds, "Making Public Schools Effective," *Social Policy*, September-October 1981, pp. 56–60.

[14] See Albert Shanker, "The End of the Traditional Model of Schooling—And a Proposal for Using Incentives to Restructure Our Public Schools," *Phi Delta Kappan*, Vol. 71, No. 5, January 1990, pp. 344–357.

[15] See Theodore R. Sizer, *Horace's Compromise: The Dilemma of the American High School*, Houghton Mifflin Company, Boston, 1984; John I. Goodlad, *A Place Called School: Prospects for the Future*, McGraw-Hill, New York, 1984, p. 229; and James P. Comer, "Educating Poor Minority Children," *Scientific American*, Vol. 259, No. 5, November 1988.

curricula. We did not set out to study site management, but we found it in the Catholic and special-purpose public schools. These schools are the unique creations of their administration and staff, as site-managed schools are supposed to be.

The focus schools' centripetal curriculum also has its counterparts in the reform literature. Oakes has argued that ability tracking stunts the development of the less-advanced students without conferring any important benefits on the more advanced.[16] The elimination of tracking has become a major agenda of minority educators, who argue that it has been used to resegregate schools and deny minority students access to the advanced language, cultural, and scientific experience they need to succeed.[17]

Schools that match our focus concept probably exist in hundreds of cities and suburbs throughout the United States. Many are public magnets that have developed a specific character so as to attract students. Others are typical religious or independent schools.[18] We will henceforth include all of these schools in our focus school concept.

Focus schooling is not a movement or a complete school of thought about the design of educational programs. It is simply a set of characteristics shared by schools that have developed their own character around a student-centered mission and a capacity to solve problems. The focus schools that we studied differed in style and sequence of instruction, and Catholic schools were quieter and more formal than some of the special-purpose public schools. But the focus schools have three important elements in common:

- They are organizations with definite missions and cultures, not simply chance aggregations of individuals who happen to be assigned to the same work site.
- Their distinct characters set them apart, in the minds of their staff, students, and parents, from other schools. Though not all focus schools have unique or highly innovative curricula, each has a special identity that inspires a sense of loyalty and common commitment.

---

[16]See Jeannie Oakes, *Keeping Track*, Yale University Press, New Haven, 1985.

[17]See Massachusetts Institute of Technology, *Education That Works: An Action Plan for the Education of Minorities*, Quality Education for Minorities Project, Cambridge, 1990.

[18]In Louisville, Ky., the public system has created three groups of schools, one patterned after Sizer's essential schools concept, one inspired by Goodlad's IDEA research, and one based on Edmonds's effective schools literature. Comer is helping school systems develop community-based schools in many cities, including New Haven, Conn., and Washington, D.C.

- They are committed to education in its broadest sense, the development of whole students. They induce values, influence attitudes, and integrate diverse sources of knowledge. They also transmit facts and impart skills, but mainly they try to mold teenagers into responsible, productive adults.

In operational terms, focus schools have the following attributes in common:

- Their clear and simple missions focus on students.
- They operate under an internal social contract that motivates discipline and academic effort.
- They are committed to parenting and to teaching practical ethics as a central part of their educational responsibility.
- Their curricula are designed to draw all students into a common core of skills and intellectual experiences.
- They consider themselves problem-solving, not program-administering, organizations.
- They work self-consciously to sustain their own capabilities and organizational character through the selection and aggressive socialization of new faculty members.
- They are accountable to the people who depend on their performance, rather than to central rule-making, auditing, or assessment organizations.

The questions of whether these features could be implemented more broadly in public schools and whether they would benefit the students that public schools now serve remain to be answered. The following sections assess whether sufficient support exists among the various actors to make focus schools more widely available to students now attending zoned schools.

V. THE CASE FOR FOCUS SCHOOLS

Can the key features of focus schools—including Catholic, special-purpose public schools, and other newly reformed models—be reproduced broadly in public secondary education? If focus-style schools become available to all public school students, will the students adjust to the greater demands and profit academically? We answer yes to both questions.

Making focus schooling broadly available is fraught with pitfalls. Some administrators and teachers may not adapt to such schools; some students may not be able to learn in such schools; many regulatory and contractual barriers exist. But there is no a priori reason why the best features of focus schools should not be available to public school students.

This section argues that focus-type schooling should be made much more broadly available in New York City and, by implication, in other major cities. It first examines criticisms of prior research on religious and special-purpose schools, including charges that observed differences in outcomes are an effect of student selectivity. It then investigates the desirability of such schools as a function of teacher, student, and administrator preferences. Finally, it turns to the feasibility of the widespread implementation of focus schools. The concluding section outlines how to proceed with widespread implementation of the principles of focus schools.

IRREPRODUCIBLE FEATURES

What explains the focus schools' relative success with their students? Some claim that school size is the most important feature; others emphasize the ability to handpick students and to expel those who do not fit in. Some claim that Catholic schools rely on unique and irreproducible features of religious education, especially the Church's moral authority, the self-confidence that teachers and administrators draw from that authority, and the dedication of priests and nuns. Others emphasize the single sex character of many Catholic schools, and the wearing of school uniforms. Finally, many traditionalists believe that the Catholic schools' success depends on regimentation of students and harsh discipline, features that are hard to sustain in a public school.

None of these features is common to all focus schools. Though individual focus schools are able to make assets of, for example, small size or single-sex education, not all focus schools have these features, nor do they derive their essential advantage over zoned schools from these features. In particular:

- Not all focus schools are small. The two largest schools in our sample were focus schools, one public and one Catholic, and they possess all of the key focus school features discussed in Sec. III.
- Many inner-city Catholic schools are dedicated to education of the poor. They consciously accept below-average students and expel fewer than 3 percent of their students each year, about the same proportion of students expelled from zoned public schools. Catholic schools traditionally accept troubled students and give them many chances to turn their lives around. Similarly, the special-purpose public schools that we studied accept a cross section of city high school students and work closely with students who were failing elsewhere.
- Catholic schools depend less and less on priests and nuns. Most teachers are lay people with lives outside the school. The schools emphasize the religious curriculum less than they did when all students were Catholic.
- The coeducational focus schools, including one Catholic school, were indistinguishable from the single-sex focus schools. And though all the Catholic schools that we studied had dress codes, the ones that required uniforms did not operate differently from those that did not. None of the special-purpose public schools required uniformity of dress.
- Not all focus schools are traditional or regimented. One of the special-purpose public schools was exceptionally open, informal, and individualized. Although all of the Catholic schools required "old fashioned" standards of behavior and studiousness, only one emphasized strong discipline and harsh punishment for infractions of rules. In all of the schools, some of the most productive classrooms were the noisiest, but the noise was connected to work rather than to distractions.

Any of these features—size, single-sex education, religious orientation—may contribute to an individual school's effectiveness. But they do not differentiate focus schools from zoned schools. A school's inability to duplicate these features does not constitute an absolute barrier to its ability to implement the essential features of focus schools.

STUDENT BODY DIFFERENCES

Although the focus schools that we visited admit disadvantaged minority students, the average student in most such schools tends to have somewhat more advantages (in terms of parental income, family stability, and parents' education) than the average student in an inner-city zoned school.[1] Moreover, even the most disadvantaged students in Catholic and special-purpose public schools have distinguished themselves by making an out-of-the-ordinary choice of schooling. On these grounds, some scholarly critics have rejected decades of research showing that schools of choice, Catholic and public magnet schools, produce superior outcomes.

Critics' concerns stem from what they call selection bias. Private and special-purpose public schools can set entry requirements, and those with large numbers of applicants can, if they want, take only the best among the qualified. Even when special-purpose public schools are forced to accept a demographic cross section of applicants, they are still able to choose from among a group that has taken the initiative to apply.

Similarly, parents who will pay tuition or seek out special schooling alternatives for their children presumably care about education more than parents who do not. At the same time, students who willingly leave their neighborhoods and friends may also be unusual in some respects. Finally, students who may have been placed against their wishes in private or special-purpose schools are likely to be surrounded by students who have sought to be there. In all of these ways, selection bias affects student composition, instructional climate, and student experience in focus schools.[2]

---

[1] In our study, the one focus school for students who had failed elsewhere was an exception. These students were below the average in income and other social advantages of even students in the zoned schools.

[2] Studies have shown that low-income and minority students do better in Catholic schools than in public schools. See especially James S. Coleman, "Private Schools, Public Schools and the Public Interest," *The Public Interest*, Vol. 64, 1981; James S. Coleman and Thomas Hoffer, *Public and Private High Schools: The Impact of Communities*, Basic Books, New York, 1987; Andrew M. Greeley, *Catholic High Schools and Minority Students*, Transaction, Inc., New Brunswick, New Jersey, 1982; James S. Coleman, Thomas Hoffer, and Sally Kilgore, *High School Achievement: Public, Catholic and Private Schools Compared*, Basic Books, New York, 1982; and Valerie E. Lee and Anthony S. Bryk, "A Multilevel Causal Model of the Social Distribution of High School Achievement," March 9, 1988, mimeograph. These studies also show, in different ways, that the gap in achievement between low-income minority students and their middle-class peers is smaller in Catholic than in public schools. Their statistics, drawn from national databases on school and student characteristics and student performance, are virtually beyond dispute. But the authors' interpretation, that the observed differences in performance between minority students in Catholic and public schools are due to the educational experiences provided by Catholic schools, has been hotly disputed. Many in the academic community questioned whether the outcomes were caused by schooling or

Measures that reduce the importance of parent and student initiative can minimize selection bias—e.g., as was done in the Partnership Program by recruitment of disadvantaged students, free tuition, and arranged transportation. But nothing short of mandatory student assignment could eliminate all possibility of such bias. Bias provides a possible alternative explanation to virtually any finding that Catholic or special-purpose public school programs make a difference.

But the fact that selection bias is an admissible explanation does not always make it the most plausible one. The Catholic school Partnership Program that we studied sought out disadvantaged minority children who would otherwise have been in zoned neighborhood public schools. Similarly, the special-purpose public schools in our sample admitted many students by lottery, and one gave preference to any student from its immediate neighborhood. Furthermore, many students in zoned public schools who exhibited interest in schooling by applying for admission to public magnets were forced to attend zoned schools because they lost out in admission lotteries. The strong demand for special-purpose public schools shows that many students would select themselves in if they could.

Based on what we saw in the course of the study, we do not believe that Catholic or special-purpose public schools would operate as smoothly—or have exactly the same level of success—if they exchanged their current student bodies for a cross section of students in zoned public schools. However, granting the validity of the concept of selection bias does not require education or public officials to reject the possibility that students now in zoned schools would do better in schools with the central features of focus schools. On the contrary, as we argue here, the number of students who could not adjust to or profit from focus schools is relatively small. And most of these students are already failing miserably in zoned schools.

This study cannot resolve the problem of selection bias. It is simply impossible to demonstrate beyond refutation that a particular school or educational approach will work for groups of students who have attended other schools and had other experiences. In the absence of a

---

by some unmeasured student characteristics, such as motivation. In 1981, an entire issue of the *Harvard Education Review* (Vol. 51, No. 4) was devoted to the dispute between Coleman and his critics. The critics essentially argued that Coleman's analysis had not—and could not—fully factor out the effects of student self-selection on student performance. Though some critics agreed that there might be a Catholic school effect, most held to the position that selection bias largely explained Catholic schools' superior outcomes. Coleman provided strong theoretical arguments for a Catholic school effect, but many researchers and school administrators continued to doubt that Catholic-style education could work for disadvantaged students or that it could be implemented in public schools. See Coleman and Hoffer (1987).

genuine experiment in which a cross section of public school students is exposed to schooling with the key features of focus schools, we cannot conclusively demonstrate the superiority of focus schooling. The final section of this report recommends such a demonstration to test the plausible hypotheses developed in the field research described in Secs. III and IV.

DESIRABILITY

From the evidence gathered in schools and from interviews with staff members and students, we conclude that:

- Near-universal dissatisfaction exists with the operation and performance of zoned schools. Administrators, teachers, students, and the broader community favor dramatic change. Further, students are now doing so badly in zoned schools that the risks of change, even wrenching change, are very low.
- Most teachers and administrators in zoned schools, rather than relying on methods and dictates from above, would prefer to have more freedom and responsibility to solve problems at the school level.
- Many teachers and administrators are willing to make the effort necessary to create a clear and fair social contract within their own school and to do their part to uphold it. (In the absence of an internal school social contract, however, administrators and teachers fear to act as they would prefer because others in the school—students, administrators, or teachers—would take advantage of them.)
- The vast majority of students now in zoned public high schools would prefer to live under a strong social contract and the leadership and guidance of adults whom they trust.
- The majority of such students could profit from high schools with simpler, centripetal curricula.

Near-Universal Dissatisfaction

No one is remotely satisfied with zoned schools' academic outcomes. Anyone who has been in the zoned schools, spending time with the many bright, imaginative students who can be found there, cannot easily accept the very low levels of current performance. One striking theme that emerged from interviews with staff and students is that the schools meet no one's needs well.

Most regard zoned schools as the result of very complex compromises—the proverbial horse designed by a committee. Many, particularly administrative staff members, believe that the schools are relatively well conceived, given the constraints and interests that they are required to satisfy. Some are justifiably proud of how well their schools cope with all the constraints imposed on them, and of how imaginative principals are in arranging the social services and material support that many students need. But no one we met would have consciously designed such a school.

Chaotic Pluralism. Zoned schools are, in effect, the result of a long series of accommodations to the interests of particular groups, diverse theories of schooling, and control measures intended to guarantee accountability to outside authorities. The essence of zoned school administration is to find a critical path among external constraints, not to create a school that best fits current students. Each constraint may have addressed a real need when it was imposed; in combination, however, the constraints sap the energy of the school and its staff.

Group interests shaping the zoned schools include:

- Externally funded programs that require the schools to differentiate among students (e.g., federal and state programs for the handicapped, the gifted, the lowest achieving).
- Board of Education rules that limit the ability of schools to select teachers.
- Union contracts that specify the hours that teachers can work and the jobs they and others can do.
- Rules guaranteeing principals life tenure in a school building.
- Board rules about the allocation of supplies and building repairs.

As discussed earlier, most staff members of zoned schools have become accustomed to seeing each other as members of interest groups to be accommodated, bargained with, or confronted. Students are treated as if they represented the clients of advocacy organizations or litigators. The principals who most want to improve their schools see that they must operate as brokers and conciliators. Rather than address the common needs in the school, they attend to the specific interests of the many groups represented in it.

Unresolved Conflicts about Instruction. Complicating the task of tending to diverse interest groups are the many distinct theories of pedagogy that zoned schools must accommodate; for example:

- Lagging students should be pulled out of regular classes for extra attention.

- Heterogeneous classes mixing high- and low-ability students retard the development of the most advanced.
- Heterogeneous classes accelerate the development of the least skilled.
- Students who have not mastered basic skills should be drilled specifically on those skills rather than taught in classes dealing with broader subject matter.
- Students' commitment to schooling will increase if they are attached to smaller affinity groups rather than to the school as a whole.
- Close measurement of school performance and sanctions for teachers and administrators whose schools are falling behind will motivate better performance.

Bureaucratic Accountability. The responsibility for external accountability appears never to end. Examples of external control measures include:

- The need to account for funds and achievement outcomes of externally funded programs (in one school each department head has to juggle student and teacher assignments to demonstrate exactly which instructional activities are supported by each of three external funding sources).
- The board's continual fine-tuning of teacher assignments to reflect changes in student attendance.
- Standardized testing programs that encourage teachers to emphasize test taking over mastery of material.
- Programs rewarding and punishing principals on the basis of their student attendance rates; such programs lead some schools to tolerate grave disruptions of the instructional process out of fear that assertive discipline would reduce attendance.

Most educators, who tend to be inherently conscientious people, might not like the rules and constraints imposed by outside authorities, but most comply nevertheless. In the process, the goals of high schools shift from using judgment on behalf of individual students to following whatever rules apply.

Many teachers and administrators believe that they are doing a good job of coping with the problems and constraints they face. Few would say that they are using their full professional abilities or performing as well as they could. The only support for current arrangements comes from a minority that believes that it has made enough career adjustments and prefers to retain current routines.

It is, of course, one thing to rail against constraints and quite another to decide which ones to remove or how to use discretion effectively. But the fact that virtually everyone considers the zoned high school an uncomfortable accommodation of conflicting demands establishes the potential for change.

Teacher and Administrator Preferences

Most administrators and teachers argue strongly for more discretion and responsibility at the school level. In fact, they appear to favor social contracts of the kinds found in focus schools, and many insist they would personally trade their current bounded responsibility for the hard work of using professional judgment on behalf of students.

But virtually all doubt the possibility of change. The situation is profoundly ironic. There is broad, if not universal, agreement about the general features of a good school. These features, described in Sec. IV, above, involve a clear mission, including an orientation to parenting and a social contract; initiative in problem solving; centripetal curriculum; socialization of teachers; and community accountability. The potential for agreement—in a sense, a latent social contract—exists.

But most faculty and staff feel powerless to change their schools. Their powerlessness is rooted in a perception of the motives and habits of others in the school. Individuals who take greater responsibility, unable to elicit reciprocal commitments from others, become isolated and burn out. The irony is that most staff members share the same preferences but appear unable to concert their efforts so as to change their schools.

Student Preferences

We found strikingly similar latent agreement among students in zoned schools. When asked which teachers and administrators they appreciated, most gave forthrightly conventional answers: They like teachers who come to class well prepared and present material clearly; they dislike teachers who act like automatons and continue with a presentation even if students fail to understand it; and they are grateful to teachers who ask questions to determine student understanding and who are willing to take a different approach if students miss the point the first time. Above all, they resent teachers who let students disrupt the class by adopting threatening or disrespectful attitudes toward the teacher or students.

Poised between childhood and adulthood, high school students are full of contradictions. The most physically mature students can be emotionally fragile; students with the bodies of children can be independent and resentful of authority. Some students appear to emphasize different aspects of their personalities on different days. High schools must decide how to deal with their students' inconsistencies.

Students in all schools showed remarkable perception about the quality of the social and physical environment. Table 4 displays the differences in student attitudes toward school conditions in each of the three types of schools. In general, focus school students believe that their schools are safer, cleaner, and more pleasant than do zoned school students. The logical connection between those perceptions and student pride and motivation is strong: Focus school students are far more likely than their zoned school counterparts to take pride in their school and consider themselves fortunate to attend it.

The attitudes and preferences of students in zoned schools surprised us. Students in zoned schools dress and present themselves differently from students in Catholic and special-purpose public schools: They are more likely to swagger and wear flashy gold jewelry, and a few will glare at a stranger. But when we asked what they wanted from their school, they gave strikingly traditional and childlike answers.

Table 4

STUDENT ATTITUDES TOWARD SCHOOL AND SCHOOL CONDITIONS[a]

	Zoned Public	Special-Purpose Public	Catholic
I feel safe in school	2.2	3.2	3.5
School is clean, in good repair	1.7	3.1	2.9
School is a nice place	1.7	2.8	2.5
I am lucky to be in this school	1.6	2.4	2.2
People say positive things about school	1.5	2.3	2.0
I am happy to be here rather than elsewhere	2.1	3.0	2.8
People take pride in school	2.0	2.6	2.3

[a]Mean responses to survey questions; 1 = almost never; 2 = occasionally; 3 = frequently; 4 = almost always. All differences are statistically significant, $p \leq .003$. See the appendix for complete survey results.

Like most other students, those in zoned schools want to be safe and cared for; they want to be treated fairly; they want, and will accept, standards consistently applied. They want to learn but cannot afford to appear to be among the few students who study or appreciate the teacher. And they want to be protected from the unruliness or dangerous behavior of their peers. Perhaps the saddest statistic in this report is the number in Table 4 showing how few zoned public school students reported, "I am lucky to be in this school."

Though many students in public schools kept us at a distance (and a few subjected us to the hostility that so discourages teachers), most talked willingly. One girl, with a sullen demeanor and a long record of fights with students and verbal abuse of teachers and administrators, admitted, "I know that people here think I am rough. But when I come to school, I feel like a little girl surrounded by hundreds of big people." Another girl told us, "You need to act tough and talk street talk or some kids will go after you. Last year I was in a class with a lot of kids who threatened you and tried to take your things. All you could do was act like you were tough and maybe would take their things."

The interviews provide a glimpse behind the students' hard shells. No individual student can afford to look like the only vulnerable member of a hardened group. They might prefer to live by conventional standards, but will adopt a menacing or rebellious attitude if they feel threatened by others. Our interviews with Partnership students corroborated this impression.

Partnership students expressed preferences very similar to those of zoned high school students. More significantly, they described the changes in their own attitude and behavior after moving from public to Catholic schools. The vast majority portrayed themselves as initially having the same rebellious attitudes that lead to poor attendance and low academic effort in public school. In their view, however, the Catholic school environment makes it acceptable for them to attend class and follow rules.

Catholic school students of both sexes said consistently that while in public school they had adopted antiacademic attitudes as a defense against other students. They reported flouting school rules, especially on discipline and attendance, because they could do it and get away with it. Teenagers in all schools seem to accept academic discipline if they cannot avoid it; when such discipline is lacking, however, they succumb to peer pressure to defy the system.[3]

---

[3]Although we did not pursue this question, these findings may be relevant in constructing a response to the findings of Berkeley anthropologist John U. Ogbu, who

One Partnership student who had attended public school the previous year said:

> I never think of staying home or cutting class now, because no one here does it. If I stayed out, the teachers would only make me come in on the weekend. It's not worth it. Last year I could stay out and nothing happened. On days when you didn't feel like coming in or you just couldn't make your hair or clothes look right, you just couldn't go to school.

A Partnership student in another school said: "Sometimes I stay up too late watching TV. Last year I'd just come to school when I woke up and got ready. This year I come in no matter how tired I am. You just can't come late here."

The following exchange demonstrates the inconsistencies and contradictions typical of these teenagers:

> Interviewer: What's the worst thing about this school?
>
> Student: This uniform. It's stupid. I'm an individual. I have my own style, know how to look good. With this I can't look the way I want. And people know I'm a Catholic school girl. They call you a bookworm, little miss brainiac.
>
> Interviewer: So you would get rid of the uniform if you could.
>
> Student: Oh no! I like it when people know where you go to school. And it's easy to get ready in the morning. You always know you look OK. Nobody has to feel bad because they can't look right.

Such inconsistencies may help to explain how students can behave so threateningly that teachers are afraid to confront them and, at the same time, prefer to live in a secure environment. They also explain how students can change so quickly in response to school structure and expectations.

FEASIBILITY OF IMPLEMENTING FOCUS SCHOOLS

Student Acceptance

As this study indicates, a very large proportion of students could benefit from a focus school. The high number of zoned school students who seek admission to magnet schools indicates the desire of many

---

reported that many minority youngsters, by the time they reach high school, have rejected school success as "acting white." The rejected behavior includes pursuing good grades, speaking standard English, and being on time. See Ogbu, "The Consequences of the American Cast System," in *The Achievement of Minority Students: New Perspectives*, U. Neisser (ed.), Lawrence Erlbaum, Hillsdale, New Jersey, 1986, pp. 19-56.

students and their families for a more structured and nurturing school environment. Citywide, several times as many students apply for seats in magnet schools as can be admitted. In the zoned schools that we visited, over 10 percent of the students had applied to magnet schools. Moreover, the vast majority of these applicants applied to eight schools, the maximum number allowed.

Students who applied to magnet schools clearly were not seeking a specific curriculum or training in a defined skill; most applied to schools offering a wide variety of academic, vocational, and arts programs. Students and counselors both agree that students apply to magnets because they and their parents want the academic emphasis and discipline, the order and structure of these schools.

The dropout rate of Partnership students—a cumulative 20 percent over four years—further indicates that a large proportion of students now in zoned schools could benefit from the approach of the focus school. Indeed, the Partnership dropout rate may be inflated because students who are intimidated by the higher expectations of the focus environment can still try less demanding zoned or alternative schools.

Student Academic Readiness

Students in zoned schools exhibit a wide range of academic skills, but most are markedly below national averages. For American-born students entering ninth grade, the cumulative effects of living in chaotic neighborhoods lead to skills levels that average more than two years below grade level. Recent immigrants may have had little schooling before reaching U.S. high schools and may enter school with little or no English and virtually no exposure to reading or mathematics. Focus schools also accept some students with similar problems, but in relatively small numbers.

Could such students profit from the enrollment and academic demands of focus schools? The answer depends, of course, on the students.

Typical students in zoned schools—those who have been in school most of the time and have a foundation in reading and mathematics but enter high school with sixth- or seventh-grade skills—probably would benefit from a focus school. Catholic and special-purpose public schools are able to expose such students to one year of skills training and integrate them into the regular curriculum by the tenth grade. Though few become excellent students, most graduate with adequate academic skills—approximately average for all high school graduates.

Students who arrive in high school virtually unschooled obviously present a much more severe problem. Many must have the intensive one- or two-year introduction to reading and arithmetic that zoned schools offer them. Some may require intensive, individually tailored instruction, and some may need the kind of group counseling that we found in the focus school for children who had failed elsewhere.

Catholic schools, which also encounter such students, as many are Catholics from Hispanic countries, premise their introduction to basic skills on the assumption that students will eventually enter the regular curriculum. Catholic schools nurture and support such students, but also require them to work extremely hard. School personnel do not shrink from telling students that they are desperately behind and can save themselves only through great effort.

For a third type of students—those with severe cognitive or emotional problems—schools with strong centripetal curricula may not work effectively. Nevertheless, as was evident in the one school in our sample that was designed for students who had failed elsewhere, most of the features of focus schools suit that population. That school reported an average daily attendance rate between 68 and 70 percent for children whose attendance while in zoned schools averaged less than 20 percent. Those students earned an average of 12 credits per year in the focus school, after averaging 4 credits per year in their zoned schools.

Children with severe problems need schools with a strong sense of mission and the capacity to adapt their programs to the students they have. Demanding academic and behavioral standards may be too challenging for such students, but the other features of focus schools— especially their commitment to mold their students' character and attitudes—are clearly appropriate.

Barriers

Even if students, teachers, and administrators individually favor the kind of schooling now available only in focus schools, would they consistently adhere to their expressed preferences? Could they create the kind of sustained cooperation such schools need to exist? Could the laws, policies, and central administrative structures that have grown up around public education tolerate the existence of large numbers of such schools?

We must recognize that many barriers exist. Inside schools, the main barriers are habits and mistrust. Students, administrators, teachers, and custodians and other service personnel must take time to learn about each other, demonstrate good faith, and settle disagreements. These actions inevitably impose costs, in the form of work and uncertainty for everyone. In public schools, as in all rule-driven organizations, people are accustomed to trading their freedom of action for the simplicity of routine. To get freedom and responsibility, people in public schools must accept the hard work of mutual confrontation and accommodation.

The external barriers to a transition are regulatory and contractual. Individual schools are now seen as branch offices of a broader institution, the school district, which itself is an instrument of the state. These larger institutions supervise extremely complex enterprises, and they are ultimately ruled by political decisionmaking bodies.

The state and the district deal with schools, and with each other, through formal policies: rules that apply to all schools; funding formulas of universal applicability; statutory programs meant to empower particular actors in the schools or to subsidize special services to defined groups; formal personnel systems that determine the assignments, responsibilities, and pay of school staff; contracts reached with staff unions; and mandated standardized assessments of school performance. The fractionation of public schools, much discussed in this and the preceding section, results directly from the ways in which the schools are governed from above.[4]

Ironically, many efforts to improve the schools from the outside have only weakened them further. Public schools have become perceptibly more formal, complex, and remote since the 1960s. The process began with regulation to ensure racial integration and equitable distribution of resources. Efforts to create teacher-proof curricula and to establish new entitlements and categorical programs for the handicapped, the gifted, and language minority groups followed.[5] The latest manifestation involves the effort to control school performance through graduation requirements, universal standardized tests, and schemes to hold schools accountable for performance indicators that are easy to measure, if not fully representative of the schools' goals.

The failure of general policy to improve schools, however, does not alter the fact that government institutions—and the general public—have responsibilities both to support the schools and to ensure that

---

[4]For discussions of the forces that pull apart zoned schools, see John E. Chubb and Terry M. Moe, "Politics, Markets, and the Organization of Schools," *American Political Science Review*, Vol. 82, No. 4, December 1988, pp. 1065–1087; Chubb and Moe, *Politics, Markets, and America's Schools*, The Brookings Institution, Washington, D.C., 1990; Jackie Kimbrough and Paul T. Hill, *The Aggregate Effects of Federal Education Programs*, The RAND Corporation, Santa Monica, Calif., R-2638-ED, September 1981; and Kimbrough and Hill, *Problems of Implementing Multiple Categorical Education Programs*, The RAND Corporation, Santa Monica, Calif., R-2957-ED, September 1983.

[5]See, for example, Arthur E. Wise, *Legislated Learning*, University of California Press, Berkeley, Calif., 1979; Kimbrough and Hill, 1981; and Arthur G. Powell, Eleanor Farrar, and David K. Cohen, *The Shopping Mall High School*, Houghton Mifflin Company, Boston, 1985.

they are performing effectively. If the key to improvement is to increase schools' internal capacity for concerted effort and effective problem solving, the challenge for policymakers and the public is to find ways to help schools without taking the initiative and professional responsibility away from teachers and principals.

In the final section, we suggest an orderly process for moving schools toward greater institutional strength without overly constraining them or abandoning responsible public oversight of their performance.

VI. RECOMMENDATIONS AND CONCLUSION

This section examines the implications of our findings about focus schools for the improvement of urban public high schools. Many educators and private citizens are now striving to make high schools work for urban minority students. Many school systems are investigating site-management plans. Thus, a real opportunity now exists for the widespread creation of focus schools.

In some cities, skepticism among teachers, administrators, parents, or school board members may engender reluctance to commit to speedy full-scale implementation of focus schools. Because of this reluctance, we also discuss ways to develop and test focus schools on a relatively small scale to permit a period of closely observed development and validation. We suggest how a school system can try a controlled limited-scale test, assess the results, and prepare for larger-scale action if the results are positive.

FOCUS SCHOOLS FOR ALL

A school system that wants to make focus schools available to all students must answer these questions:

- Who has to agree to initiate the widespread development of focus schools, and how can they come to agreement?
- What do they have to agree to and what must they avoid?
- How can true focus schools be created?
- How can educators and the public judge whether focus schools are developing properly and are helping their students?

Who Must Agree

Because focus-style public schools already exist in New York City and other major cities, obviously no absolute barriers exist to their creation. But focus schools are now treated as exceptions to the normal pattern of school governance. The parties to an agreement to make focus schools available to all students must include the state department of education, the superintendent of schools (in New York City, the chancellor), the board of education, and the teachers' union (in New York City, the United Federation of Teachers).

Because the educational initiative in most cities belongs to the superintendent or chancellor, he or she should propose the reform, suggest its outline, and provide a forum for negotiation with the other principal parties. But the negotiations should be conducted in public, so that those inclined to erect barriers will be accountable to business and civic leaders and parents who want the schools reformed.

What They Should Agree to and What They Must Avoid

To develop properly, focus schools will need a delegation of budgetary and staffing decisions to the school-site level, as is being attempted in Dade County, Florida; Rochester, New York; Prince William County, Virginia; and Edmonton, Alberta. In these places, the four agencies named above have agreed to relax the rules that constrain schools in an effort to strengthen individual schools as organizations. New York City and other major cities must achieve the same agreement in principle. Teachers and administrators at the school-site level cannot be expected to risk their work routines and comfortably delineated roles if people above them are unwilling to do the same.

All parties must agree to waive any general rules and policies that seriously impede the development of focus schools. Consistent with the requirement that focus schools must be strong organizations with their own distinctive character, they must not be micromanaged from above. An organization that has been crushed by regulation, contracts, artificial incentive schemes, and reporting requirements cannot be improved by more of the same. Great symbolic initiatives and sweeping new mandates cannot create focus schools. Quiet work at the school level can.

Creation of New Focus Schools

Focus schools are distinctive, largely self-governing organizations capable of solving problems on their own and taking responsibility for the results. They fit the general rubric of the popular movement toward site-based management in public education. But site management alone will not create focus schools.

As site management is practiced in most places (and as it has been proposed for New York City), it promises to accomplish little beyond transferring the politics of interest group negotiations from the school district to the school building. It encourages interest bargaining among staff members, not governance of the school according to a strong central principle.

Site management decentralizes some decisions to the school level and mandates that issues will be decided through open bargaining among teachers, administrators, and (frequently) parents. It normally starts with an existing zoned school community and invites the members to negotiate about the issues that concern them. Naturally enough, the issues that concern staff members—their working conditions and the respective rights and duties of the principal and teachers—are the main topics of discussion in most site-managed schools.

A focus school is site managed, but with a difference. It is built around specific educational and ethical principles that guide the selection of faculty and the socialization of staff and students. The principles can never be so explicit as to cover all decisions, but the fact that all members of the school community have been selected and socialized on the same basis influences the character of issues that arise for decision and the manner of their resolution. The school's basic principles guide all bargaining and decisionmaking; the ultimate standard is whether an action promotes the school's basic mission, not whether it accommodates the interests of all parties.

A focus school can be built around various principles, e.g., serving a particular business community, using arts education to motivate children's learning of basic skills, implementing Sizer's educational ideas, preparing minority children for positions of community leadership, nurturing potential Talmudic scholars, or implementing the precepts of St. Ignatius. But it must have a principle of some kind.

Because existing zoned schools are diverse and fragmented by design, it is difficult to imagine how strong agreements on principle could emerge within them. Focus schools are much more likely to develop from the ground up, around a small core of individuals who are committed to a particular principle and are permitted to build and influence a staff and student body.

Focus schools should therefore be built up from a small cadre, rather than superimposed on an existing school. An effort to create focus schools should proceed from the following seven premises:

1. Focus schools must be constructed by the staff members who will work in them.

The capacities to solve problems, to sustain an internal social contract, and to remain accountable to those who depend on the school's performance require a strong organization, not one that is dominated by externally imposed rules and procedures. The defining characteristics of a focus school should be established in advance, as they have been in the schools analyzed in this report. But the implementation of the focus concept in a particular school, including decisions about style of pedagogy and school climate, should be established at the school level, in light of the needs of the specific students to be served.

2. The realization of the focus school concept requires some a priori demonstration of school staff good faith.

A small cadre, consisting at a minimum of a principal and a lead teacher, must accept the basic goal of building a school with the features defined above and making it work for students, including educationally disadvantaged minority students. The cadre should select other faculty and staff members on the basis of their technical competence and acceptance of the school's basic principles. Once the staff is assembled, decisions should be made as collegially as possible, but governed by the initial "constitution" developed by the cadre and used as the basis for staff recruitment.[1]

3. Some mechanism must be devised to enable staff and students to sort themselves among focus schools.

As we observed in Catholic and special-purpose public schools, choice allows schools to create and maintain their distinctive character. Individuals can leave rather than dissent; people whose preferences might be in the minority in several schools can be united into a majority in a single school reflecting their preferences.

Large numbers of focus high schools can exist in New York City only if staff members and students can choose where they will teach and learn. But choice is simply a necessary element of a movement toward focus schools, not the whole reform itself. The effort to create focus schools is one leg of the reform effort; choice is the other. As schools develop into strong organizations with character, commitment to mission, and definite educational approaches, parents and students

---

[1]The process of creating new participatory organizations grounded on specific principles has been carefully developed in private industry. Though it is possible to restructure an existing organization, restructuring is accomplished more easily, and typically with greater success, by creating new organizations on principles that all participants understand and support. As Coleman describes the development of new participatory manufacturing plants, cadres are formed to develop statements of goals and operating styles for a new organization, and to recruit others on the basis of their technical competence and willingness to accept the newly constructed "constitution." Many of the constitutions thus developed are simple and hard to distinguish from those of other plants similarly developed. But the fact that the mission and decisionmaking processes were developed in the plant, and by the people who will work in it, sets the stage for worker participation and high performance. See James S. Coleman, *Foundations of Social Theory*, The Belknap Press of Harvard University Press, Cambridge, Mass., 1990, p. 437.

will come to understand their differences, and they must be free to choose among them.

Once schools have the chance to develop a sense of common purpose and reciprocal obligation among students, faculty, administration, and parents, choice facilitates their continuation. It ensures that students will learn in an environment that they believe can help them and that teachers will work in a school whose goals and approaches they can support. Choice also means that people who do not fit where they find themselves can search for alternatives, rather than disrupting arrangements that work for others. But choice alone, without a prior effort to create strong, mission-oriented schools, will produce only confusion and disappointment.

Free movement of students and teachers can accomplish little in a system with a few highly regarded schools and many weak ones. Schools with good reputations become oversubscribed, and most students are forced to attend the very schools that they are trying to escape. This is, in fact, the case in New York City today. Many of the best magnet high schools have over 30 times as many applicants as spaces; most students who apply to magnets lose out in the lottery and must enroll in the zoned school they sought to leave.

The concept of supply and demand explains the situation aptly. Choice is the perfect mechanism for the expression of demand: Like money in the hands of consumers, choice creates the opportunity for people to buy what they want if they can find it. But purchasing power has little meaning if there are no attractive goods to choose. In theory, purchasing power stimulates supply: Entrepreneurs sensing an unmet demand will invest in efforts to provide what people will buy.

In the real world, however, entrepreneurs are constrained by the limits of their own expertise and by the difficulty of producing what consumers want. In the case of good inner-city schools, few people know how to produce them, and the best evidence is that they must be carefully built one by one, not mass produced. Demand alone cannot produce good inner-city schools. The unfulfilled demand has been there for years.

An effort to create many focus schools, each with its individual character and appeal to students and teachers, is the core of any reform. That effort must be made, not brushed aside as a detail that will be taken care of by the operation of a free market.

4. Though most focus schools should aim to serve a cross section of city high school students, some schools should target students who have failed in other settings.

Most of our focus schools were college preparatory, but one had a special mission of serving students who had failed in other settings as a result of health, emotional, legal, or family problems. This school had all the defining characteristics of focus schools, but it provided more intensive counseling and a slower-paced core curriculum than the other focus schools. Despite the fact that they were adversely selected, i.e., assigned to the school because of their prior difficulties in regular schools, students attained better attendance records and graduated at a higher rate than students in the zoned schools.

Such outcomes demonstrate the influence that a focus school can exert on students. They also demonstrate the value of having a range of focus schools to deal with student needs. In general, a range of focus schools with complementary missions would probably serve students far better than a group of identical but highly complex institutions, each meant to fill needs of virtually all students.

5. Planning for the inevitability of a period of organizational trial and error is essential.

The actual construction of a specific focus school must be worked out to fit the personalities, abilities, and needs of staff, students, and community. The social contract, in particular, can be established in the beginning through subscription, i.e., by the agreement of individual staff and students to accept an established set of mutual obligations. But the social contract has meaning only if it is a living agreement—like a constitution, amenable to change but seldom changed.

The transformation of an agreement in principle into a living agreement takes time, and no school should be expected to have all the attributes of a mature focus school overnight. Even the Catholic schools, which have the advantage of a well-known social contract and a huge body of thoroughly socialized potential adherents, expect new schools to take two or three years to establish a stable identity and efficient self-management.

6. The central office must change to complement the new site-managed schools.

The central office must become less a regulatory and evaluative organization and more a facilitator of school-level problem solving. It must, in short, increase its capacities to (1) help schools to become strong and distinctive institutions; (2) provide specialized services that no single school can afford (e.g., special education); (3) find the expert help schools need to solve problems; (4) facilitate the choice process so that staff and students can be in schools whose missions and social contracts are compatible with their tasks and needs; (5) protect the concept of problem-solving schools by intervening to help failing schools, not by creating new regulations to prevent the occasional failure; and (6) create publications and forums through which the staffs of focus schools can share promising ideas and strategies and parents can learn about the options available to their children.

    7. Focus schools cannot be mass produced.

The Catholic and special-purpose public schools in our sample were unique creations, built one at a time. The enormous institutional resources on which a big-city public school system can draw may mean that many such individual efforts can be mounted simultaneously, but the shortcut of mandating standard approaches will only fail. Staff cadres commissioned to build focus schools should not have to act like mass-production engineers who duplicate a fixed model as efficiently as possible. They should have the time and external support needed to transform a general concept into a plan that fits the circumstances of their own students and staff.

With these premises as a guide, any city can develop focus schools. The program should have two parts: the establishment of focus schools and an objective assessment of their institutional development and student outcomes.

Implementation

Two options exist for creating focus schools: the organization of schools with a specific philosophy or the creation of new programs to be housed in existing buildings and serve an existing student body.

Entirely New Schools. In theory, the simplest way to create a focus high school would be to start with a new or unoccupied building and to recruit a staff and principal specifically to do the job. Principals and lead teachers could be recruited through requests for proposals, as was done in Dade County, Florida.

Proposals could be evaluated in terms of demonstrated understanding of the focus concept and a plausible description of the basic educational and ethical principles that would guide the school's effort to serve its students. Once selected, school staff could publish a prospectus describing the school's goals and expected organization and then select staff from among those who applied to work specifically in the school. After a period of planning—Dade County took one year—the staff would occupy a school site and accept students.

This approach would give school staff a chance to form working relationships and plan programs before they had to deal with students.

Because staff presumably would not have worked together before, they would have relatively little need to break old habits or root out features in conflict with the mission of the focus school.

Schools on Sites of Existing Zoned Schools. Establishing new focus schools in buildings now occupied by zoned schools is a more complex undertaking, but it may be the only possible course. Because dedicated buildings may not be available and because students' education must not be interrupted, focus schools may have to develop inside zoned schools. Focus schools could begin as small schools inside zoned schools, accepting students by lottery or serving only, say, ninth graders in the first year and gradually growing to serve the whole student population.

As in the case of entirely new schools, the process should start with the selection of volunteer core staff members, at least a principal and a lead teacher. Selection could be made through requests for proposals or by central office nomination of qualified teachers and administrators who have expressed interest in building focus schools. The principal and lead teacher should spend a year's planning time recruiting teachers and administrators for their school-within-a-school. The school staff should be expanded with recruits and volunteers until, after approximately four years, the zoned school would disappear.

Though the student population need not shift during the transition from zoned to focus school, the faculty and administrative staff should change. To prevent an inadvertent return to the practices of the former zoned school, few teachers and administrators should remain in the same building. Even those who volunteer to work in focus schools should transfer to other new focus schools. These changes are possible, of course, only with the enthusiastic cooperation of teacher professional organizations.

Assessing the Results

The key test is simply whether focus schools can indeed develop through the gradual processes of recruitment and expansion described above. If such schools can develop, recruit staff, and retain students who have the freedom to choose other schools, the basic case will have been made. In addition to simple survival, finer measures of internal health would include teacher morale, job turnover, and student attendance.

Another issue is whether focus schools can outlast the political and regulatory pressures for standardization and control by external mandates. Special-purpose focus schools now survive despite heavy political and regulatory pressures, but they require charismatic and politically astute leadership. If public focus schools are to become widely available, the environment must be supportive enough to permit them to survive without extraordinarily gifted leadership. Superintendents and school boards must resist the political and regulatory pressure to recreate the zoned school if focus schools are to expand.

The final issue is whether focus schools will be able to draw and succeed in educating a true cross section of the city school population. If the focus schools fail to attract and retain large numbers of less advantaged students, the schools will have failed this test. We do not believe that they will fail, however, if the range of focus schools developed includes some schools for troubled students. Such schools must offer the counseling and slower pacing that these students need, without relaxing the ultimate goal of mastery of traditional high school material.

The current performance of zoned schools supplies an appropriate minimum standard for the assessment of new focus schools. Once focus schools have developed, the following questions must be answered:

- Do the disadvantaged minority students who would otherwise attend inner-city zoned schools attend more regularly, experience fewer disciplinary or behavioral problems, graduate in higher proportions, take more challenging classes, enter institutions of higher education in higher numbers, and score better on consequential standardized tests such as the SAT when they attend focus schools?
- Do they adapt more readily to the discipline of work and higher education so that employers and college admissions officers believe that they are better prepared than their older brothers and sisters?

Higher standards, such as those advocated by the New York State Regents or the National Governors Conference, should motivate further improvement efforts. But they should not be the first standards that focus schools are required to meet.

A MORE CAUTIOUS APPROACH

Educational and civic leaders in some cities may be encouraged by the evidence presented here but be unable to gain support for a major effort to replace zoned schools with focus schools. In that case, a more cautious incremental approach may be necessary. We briefly outline such an approach, which is based on the idea of a controlled test followed by assessment of results and replication of successful models.

A test should be small, initially involving three to ten high schools. It should last long enough for schools to be able to define their individual characters, stabilize staff and curriculum, and have measurable effects on students. A period of four or five years would enable some students to spend an entire high school career in a focus school and provide some leeway for false starts by the focus school.

Focus schools developed for the test should fit into the normal funding constraints of the city's public high schools. The question of reproducibility can be answered only if focus schools must operate on the same per pupil budgets as zoned schools.

Focus schools should not, however, have to pay the financial or transaction costs of central office supervisory functions that they inherently do not need. The central office should agree up front to an absolute limit on its financial and record-keeping demands, so that school staff need not bear the double burden of making decisions at the site level and responding to all the bureaucratic imperatives that have grown up around zoned schools.

As in the case of a full-scale districtwide attempt to develop focus schools, the test should have a definite assessment component. Focus schools should meet the tests described above: Do they stabilize in character, attract and retain staff, and attract a cross section of the district population, including students now served by zoned high schools in low-income areas? Do they serve those students better than the current zoned schools?

Finally, the superintendent, board, teachers' union, and other parties interested in reform, particularly the business community, should also agree in advance to give the test a fair chance to succeed and to accept the results if they are positive. If focus schools prove feasible and beneficial to students, the city should be able to expand their numbers relatively quickly. Experienced teachers and administrators from the focus schools established for the test could serve as mentors for new focus school staffs. New focus schools should continue to start modestly and expand within a few years to serve all students in formerly zoned schools.

CONCLUSION

The actions urged in this report complement other reforms now being urged for public schools. This report shows how public schools can be built to incorporate the characteristics that Catholic and special-purpose public schools have developed to work with disadvantaged minority students. The two other major reforms now being urged—choice and site-based management—address real problems, but as we have argued, neither, by itself or in combination, will create dramatic improvement in inner-city schools. Site-based management enables staff to tailor their school to the specific needs of its students; when given the freedom to govern themselves, however, staffs of existing schools too often bog down in negotiations about their own working conditions. Choice ensures that staff and teachers can leave schools that they do not like; but it does not guarantee that demand will elicit a supply of good schools, especially in inner cities. But with the addition of the focus school concept, choice and site-based management can become powerful engines for the reform of inner-city schools.

In an earlier RAND report, the authors characterized public school reform as a double helix, involving both an outside strategy for creating the conditions that make school improvement possible and an inside strategy for transforming the schools as institutions.[2] Choice and the deregulation that accompany site-based management create the external conditions for effective schools. The focus school approach develops the internal strategy. It shows how schools themselves can become institutions that motivate, lead, and teach disadvantaged inner-city youth.

---

[2]See Paul T. Hill, Arthur E. Wise, and Leslie Shapiro, *Educational Progress: Cities Mobilize to Improve Their Schools*, The RAND Corporation, Santa Monica, Calif., R-3711-JSM/CSTP, January 1989, p. 11.

Appendix

STUDENT SURVEY PROCEDURES AND RESULTS

Lisa Hudson

PURPOSE AND DESIGN

The student survey questionnaire reproduced at the end of this appendix was given to 317 students in three Catholic schools, two zoned public schools, and two special-purpose public schools, and the results analyzed. Table A.1 shows the sample sizes and basic characteristics of students from each type of school.

RESULTS

Responses to the 52 survey items assessing school conditions were divided into seven topic areas: clarity of mission; perception and consequences of school conditions; atmosphere for learning; care for students; equitable treatment; challenge/push for learning; and future expectations. Table A.2 lists the items by section, and the mean student scores for each item in each type of school. For each item, variance was analyzed to test the significance of the mean differences

Table A.1

SIZE AND CHARACTERISTICS OF SURVEY SAMPLE, BY SCHOOL TYPE

	Zoned Public	Special-Purpose Public	Catholic
Number of students surveyed	75	85	157
Average age	16.5	15.1	16.1
Percentage female	50.7	68.4	58.6
Percentage with two parents who completed high school[a]	55.7	85.0	68.5

[a]These data should be interpreted with caution, as this item had a very high nonresponse rate of 19 percent, 29 percent, and 17 percent, respectively, for each school type.

Table A.2

MEAN RESPONSES TO SCHOOL SURVEY, BY SCHOOL TYPE*

	Zoned Public	Special-Purpose Public	Catholic	ANOVA** Significance Level
CLARITY OF RULES AND MISSION				
You get the sense that everyone at this school is working toward the same goal.	2.1	2.6	2.5	$p = .010$
SCHOOL PRIDE AND CONDITIONS				
I feel safe in the halls of this school.	2.2	3.2	3.5	$p < .001$***
The school building is kept clean and in good repair.	1.7	3.1	2.9	$p < .001$***
This school is a nice place to spend the day.	1.7	2.8	2.5	$p < .001$***
When people find out that I go to this school, they think I am lucky.	1.6	2.4	2.2	$p < .001$***
When people who don't go here say things about this school, they say positive things.	1.5	2.3	2.0	$p < .001$***
When I compare it to other schools that I might go to in New York, I am happy that I am at this school.	2.1	3.0	2.8	$p < .001$***
People who go here take pride in the school.	2.0	2.6	2.3	$p = .003$
ATMOSPHERE FOR LEARNING				
Attendance here is good; students come to school and go to class.	1.8	2.6	3.1	$p < .001$***
Students here act respectfully toward the school.	1.6	2.5	2.5	$p < .001$***
Students here act respectfully toward the teachers.	1.8	2.6	2.7	$p < .001$***
Students here are happy enough just to pass; they don't worry about doing well.	3.1	2.4	2.6	$p < .001$***
Students here think it's a good thing to do well in school; they won't think you're uncool just because you get good grades.	2.4	2.8	2.9	$p < .001$***
Students here take the rules seriously.	1.8	2.4	2.1	$p = .001$***
Students here work hard at schoolwork.	2.4	2.8	2.4	$p = .005$
This school makes students want to learn.	2.3	2.9	2.7	$p = .012$
Students here act respectfully toward one another.	2.2	2.5	2.6	$p = .043$
Most students here do most of the homework assigned to them.	2.2	2.5	2.4	$p = .204$

Table A.2 (continued)

	Zoned Public	Special-Purpose Public	Catholic	ANOVA** Significance Level
CARE FOR STUDENTS				
When new students come here, they feel welcome.	2.2	2.8	2.5	p = .015
If something is really going wrong for a student here, one of the faculty members will notice and talk to the student about it.	2.9	2.7	3.0	p = .116
People here feel as if they are part of a community.	2.3	2.5	2.5	p = .455
The principal here really cares about the students.	3.0	2.8	2.9	p = .463
Teachers here go out of their way to help you understand.	2.9	2.7	2.8	p = .523
I feel like most of the faculty here really want to help me learn and grow.	2.8	2.9	3.0	p = .590
The rules here make sense and exist for good reasons.	2.7	2.6	2.4	p = .088
The rules here are enforced fairly; no one gets special treatment.	2.3	2.5	2.6	p = .446
EQUITABLE TREATMENT				
The teachers here only call on a few of their favorites; the rest of the class just ends up sitting there.	2.5	1.6	2.2	p < .001***
If you're really smart or dumb, the teachers pay attention to you, but if you're average, you tend to fall through the cracks.	2.0	2.3	2.3	p = .265
There are interesting classes here that I bet I could do well in that the school won't let me take.	2.1	2.3	2.4	p = .340
CHALLENGE/PUSH FOR LEARNING				
Teachers here are satisfied as long as you pass; they don't care so much about your really learning or doing well.	2.5	1.9	1.8	p < .001***
Classes here are challenging and interesting.	2.4	2.8	2.7	p = .083
If you don't do your homework, you're likely to be penalized.	2.2	2.5	2.7	p = .019
Teachers here expect me to succeed.	3.1	3.4	3.4	p = .091
In classes here, teachers try to make you think for yourself.	3.0	3.1	3.1	p = .608
The expectations people have for me here make me want to try my hardest.	2.8	2.9	3.0	p = .677
Teachers assign homework that is more than just busy work; it is a chance for you to think and learn on your own.	2.8	2.9	2.9	p = .830

Table A.2 (continued)

	Zoned Public	Special-Purpose Public	Catholic	ANOVA** Significance Level
FUTURE ORIENTATION				
Students here think they'll probably graduate from high school.	2.9	3.4	3.6	p < .001***
Students here think they'll probably go to college.	2.5	3.1	3.1	p < .001***
When students here make decisions, they think about how they will affect their future.	2.4	2.8	2.7	p = .214

*Means represent responses to a four-point scale, with 1 = almost never, 2 = occasionally, 3 = frequently, and 4 = almost always.
**Analysis of variance.
***Significant at .05 level after Bonferroni correction for multiple comparisons.

among school types. The last column in Table A.2 lists the significance level (p-value) for the analysis of variance (ANOVA) test; p-values at or below .001 are statistically significant after applying a Bonferroni correction for multiple comparisons.[1]

Table A.2 shows an interesting pattern of results. Students in the three types of schools do not perceive statistically significant differences in the care and concern faculty show toward students, in the equitable distribution of attention and curriculum, or in the clarity of school rules. The lack of differences on the latter two measures is not surprising for two reasons. First, the survey items on equitable treatment and clarity of school rules and mission are probably somewhat weak measures of these constructs, and second, students probably have little real sense of the level of clarity and equality that exists at the school level. The fairly consistent and positive ratings on the items assessing school faculties' concern for students reflect favorably on the degree to which personnel in schools of all types attend to students' social and/or emotional needs.

In contrast, the results indicate large and fairly consistent differences in how students in zoned public schools view school conditions and levels of pride in their school, the atmosphere for learning that exists in their school, and their future. On every item in these categories, zoned public school students rank themselves and/or their schools lower—typically significantly lower—than do students in either special-purpose public schools or Catholic schools.

In terms of school atmosphere, significant differences appeared in six of the ten items in this group—school attendance, student respect for school, student respect for teachers, student effort, students' view of doing well, and taking school rules seriously. On each of these items, Catholic and special-purpose public schools were given, on average, a neutral or positive rating, while zoned public schools were given mostly negative ratings.

The same pattern applies to the seven items assessing school pride and conditions, where zoned schools ranked significantly lower on six of the seven items. On the "future orientation" items, students in

---

[1] A correction for multiple comparisons is necessary because more than one mean difference (in this case, 39 mean differences) is being tested. To understand why this correction is necessary, consider the following situation: Using the traditional p-value of null hypothesis of no difference; thus, 100 tests will yield (on average) five falsely significant results. The Bonferroni correction adjusts the significance level so that the probability of rejecting a true null hypothesis applies to the full set of comparisons. In this case, we use an adjusted p-value of $.05/39=.0013$; the chances of labeling a nonsignificant result as significant is now only 5 percent across all comparisons (and only .13 percent for each comparison).

zoned public schools were less likely to believe that their classmates planned to graduate or go on to college than were students in Catholic or special-purpose public schools. However, students in all three types of schools felt that their peers were not especially likely to consider how their decisions affect their futures; students may not have always understood the types of decisions implied by this item.

The data on the degree of "challenge," or the "push for learning," in each type of school are less consistent. Again, Catholic and special-purpose public schools appear to be virtually identical, while zoned public schools are consistently ranked less favorably, even though the difference is statistically significant on only one of the seven items in this group. It is unclear why this item—"Teachers here are satisfied as long as you pass; they don't care so much about your really learning or doing well"—should show a significant difference, while other items on teachers' expectations do not; however, it seems likely that this item most directly taps the "message" that students receive about what their school expects from them (and, by implication, thinks they are capable of).

In sum, these data show a remarkable similarity between Catholic schools and special public schools, with students typically giving these schools a neutral or positive ranking on the measures included in our survey. Zoned public schools, in contrast, were ranked less highly on many measures, particularly on measures of school pride, school conditions in general, the atmosphere for learning at the school, and the degree to which students plan to continue their education.

STUDENT SURVEY

This survey consists of a list of statements that are true in some schools. We want to know how well each of them describes your school. They may be true almost never, occasionally, frequently, or almost always. Please use the following scale:

    1: Almost never
    2: Occasionally
    3: Frequently
    4: Almost always

1. When people find out that I go to this school, they think I am lucky.   1 2 3 4

2. When people who don't go here say things about this school, they say positive things.   1 2 3 4

3. When I compare it to other schools that I might go to in New York, I am happy that I am at this school.   1 2 3 4

4. This school makes students want to learn.   1 2 3 4

5. People who go here take pride in the school.   1 2 3 4

6. Attendance here is good; students come to school and go to class.   1 2 3 4

7. Students here act respectfully toward the school.   1 2 3 4

8. Students here act respectfully toward the teachers.   1 2 3 4

9. Students here act respectfully toward one another.   1 2 3 4

10. The principal here really cares about the students.   1 2 3 4

11. If something is really going wrong for a student here, one of the faculty members will notice and talk to the student about it.   1 2 3 4

12. I feel like most of the faculty here really want to help me learn and grow.   1 2 3 4

13. Teachers here go out of their way to help you understand.   1 2 3 4

14. In classes here, teachers try to make you think for yourself.   1 2 3 4

15.	Classes here are challenging and interesting.	1 2 3 4
16.	Teachers assign homework that is more than just busy work; it is a chance for you to think and learn on your own.	1 2 3 4
17.	If you don't do your homework, you're likely to be penalized.	1 2 3 4
18.	Most students here do most of the homework assigned to them.	1 2 3 4
19.	Teachers here are satisfied as long as you pass; they don't care so much about your really learning or doing well.	1 2 3 4
20.	Teachers here expect me to succeed.	1 2 3 4
21.	The expectations people have for me here make me want to try my hardest.	1 2 3 4
22.	The rules here make sense and exist for good reasons.	1 2 3 4
23.	The rules here are enforced fairly; no one gets special treatment.	1 2 3 4
24.	Students here take the rules seriously.	1 2 3 4
25.	Students here think they'll probably graduate from high school.	1 2 3 4
26.	Students here think they'll probably go to college.	1 2 3 4
27.	When students here make decisions, they think about how they will affect their future.	1 2 3 4
28.	Students here work hard at schoolwork.	1 2 3 4
29.	Students here think it's a good thing to do well in school; they won't think you're uncool just because you get good grades.	1 2 3 4
30.	Students here are happy enough just to pass; they don't worry about doing well.	1 2 3 4
31.	If you're really smart or dumb, the teachers pay attention to you, but if you're average, you tend to fall through the cracks.	1 2 3 4
32.	The teachers here only call on a few of their favorites; the rest of the class just ends up sitting there.	1 2 3 4

33. There are interesting classes here that I bet I could do well in that the school won't let me take.   1 2 3 4
34. People here feel as if they are part of a community.   1 2 3 4
35. When new students come here, they feel welcome.   1 2 3 4
36. You get the sense that everyone at this school is working toward the same goal.   1 2 3 4
37. I feel safe in the halls of this school.   1 2 3 4
38. The school building is kept clean and in good repair.   1 2 3 4
39. This school is a nice place to spend the day.   1 2 3 4

We need to know a little bit about you and your family to help us with our study. Please answer the following questions.

40. What is your age?   12 13 14 15 16 17 18 19 20 21
41.   grade?   9 10 11 12
42.   sex?   M F
43. How many years have you been at this high school? _____
44. Where did you go to school before you came here? (List all schools since sixth grade.)
45. What do you want to do after you leave high school?
46. What do you do in the afternoons after school?
47. How many brothers and sisters do you have?   _____
48. How many are in elementary or secondary school, or haven't started school yet?   _____
49. How many have graduated from high school?   _____
50. How many had to leave high school without finishing?   _____
51. What is the highest grade your mother was able to complete?

    1 2 3 4 5 6 7 8 9 10 11 12
    Some college   College degree

52 What is the highest grade your father was able to complete?

    1 2 3 4 5 6 7 8 9 10 11 12
    Some college   College degree

BIBLIOGRAPHY

Abramowitz, Susan, and E. Ann Stackhouse, *The Private High School Today*, National Institute of Education, Washington, D.C., December 1980.

Bryk, Anthony S., "Disciplined Inquiry or Policy Argument?" *Harvard Educational Review*, Vol. 51, 1981, pp. 497–509.

Cain, Glen G., and Arthur S. Goldberger, "Public and Private Schools Revisited," *Sociology of Education*, Vol. 56, October 1983, pp. 209–218.

Camarena, Margaret M., "A Comparison of the Organizational Structures of Public and Catholic High Schools," dissertation, Stanford University, August 1986.

——, "A Comparison of the Instructional Practices of Public & Catholic Schools," mimeograph, University of Washington, n.d.

——, "Following the Right Track: A Comparison of Tracking Practices in Public & Catholic Schools," mimeograph, n.d.

Carnegie Institution, *A Nation Prepared*, Forum on Education and the Economy, Washington, D.C., 1986.

Chubb, John E., and Terry M. Moe, "Politics, Markets, and the Organization of Schools," *American Political Science Review*, Vol. 82, No. 4, December 1988, pp. 1065–1087.

——, *Politics, Markets, and America's Schools*, The Brookings Institution, Washington, D.C., 1990.

Cibulka, James G., Timothy J. O'Brien, and Donald Zewe, *Inner City Private Elementary Schools*, Marquette University Press, Milwaukee, 1982.

Coleman, James S., "Private Schools, Public Schools and the Public Interest," *The Public Interest*, Vol. 64, 1981.

——, *Foundations of Social Theory*, The Belknap Press of Harvard University Press, Cambridge, Mass., 1990.

Coleman, James S., and Thomas Hoffer, *Public and Private High Schools: The Impact of Communities*, Basic Books, New York, 1987.

Coleman, James S., Thomas Hoffer, and Sally Kilgore, "Public and Private Schools," National Center for Education Statistics, National Opinion Research Center, Chicago, 1981.

——, *High School Achievement: Public, Catholic and Private Schools Compared*, Basic Books, New York, 1982.

———, "Cognitive Outcomes in Public and Private Schools," *Sociology of Education*, Vol. 55, April/July 1982, pp. 65–76.
Comer, James P., "Educating Poor Minority Children," *Scientific American*, Vol. 259, No. 5, November 1988.
DiPrete, Thomas A., et al., "Discipline and Order in American High Schools," National Opinion Research Center, Chicago, November 1981.
Edmonds, Ronald R., "Making Public Schools Effective," *Social Policy*, September-October 1981, pp. 56–60.
Firestone, William A., and Sheila Rosenblum, "Building Commitment in Urban High Schools," *Educational Evaluation and Policy Analysis*, Vol. 10, No. 4, Winter 1988, pp. 285–299.
Foley, Eileen, and Peggy Crull, "Educating the At-Risk Adolescent," Public Education Association, n.d.
Foster, Gail Edghill, "Guest Editorial. Cultivating the Thinking Skills of Low Achievers: A Matter of Equity," *Journal of Negro Education*, Vol. 58, No. 4, 1989, pp. 461–467.
Gold, Martin, and David W. Mann, *Expelled to a Friendlier Place: A Study of Effective Alternative Schools*, University of Michigan Press, Ann Arbor, 1984.
Goldberger, Arthur S., and Glen G. Cain, "The Causal Analysis of Cognitive Outcomes in the Coleman, Hoffer and Kilgore Report," *Sociology of Education*, Vol. 55, April/July 1982, pp. 103–122.
Goodlad, John I., *A Place Called School: Prospects for the Future*, McGraw-Hill, New York, 1984.
Greeley, Andrew M., *The Education of Catholic Americans*, Aldine, Chicago, 1966.
———, "Who Controls Catholic Education?" *Education and Urban Society*, Vol. 9, 1977, pp. 146–166.
———, *Catholic High Schools and Minority Students*, Transaction, Inc., New Brunswick, New Jersey, 1982.
Harvard Educational Review, Vol. 51, No. 4, 1981.
Hill, Paul T., Arthur E. Wise, and Leslie Shapiro, *Educational Progress: Cities Mobilize to Improve Their Schools*, The RAND Corporation, Santa Monica, Calif., R-3711-JSM/CSTP, January 1989.
Hoffer, Thomas, Andrew M. Greeley, and James S. Coleman, "Achievement Growth in Public and Catholic Schools," *Sociology of Education*, Vol. 58, April 1985, pp. 74–97.
Hudolin, Janet M., "The Social Organization of an Urban Catholic School: Policy Implications for Public Schools," master's thesis, University of Michigan, August 1989.

Jensen, Gary F., "Explaining Differences in Academic Behavior Between Public School and Catholic School Students: A Quantitative Case Study," *Sociology of Education*, Vol. 59, January 1986, pp. 32–41.
Kimbrough, Jackie, and Paul T. Hill, *The Aggregate Effects of Federal Education Programs*, The RAND Corporation, Santa Monica, Calif., R-2638-ED, September 1981.
——, *Problems of Implementing Multiple Categorical Education Programs*, The RAND Corporation, Santa Monica, Calif., R-2957-ED, September 1983.
Koretz, Daniel, "Arriving in Lake Wobegon: Are Standardized Tests Exaggerating Achievement and Distorting Instruction?" *American Educator*, Summer 1988, pp. 8–15.
Lee, Valerie E., and Anthony S. Bryk, "A Multilevel Causal Model of the Social Distribution of High School Achievement," March 9, 1988, mimeograph.
——, "Curriculum Tracking as Mediating the Social Distribution of High School Achievement," *Sociology of Education*, Vol. 61, April 1988, pp. 78–94.
Massachusetts Institute of Technology, *Education That Works: An Action Plan for the Education of Minorities*, Quality Education for Minorities Project, Cambridge, 1990.
McCord, Colin, M.D., and Harold P. Freeman, M.D., "Excess Mortality in Harlem," *New England Journal of Medicine*, Vol. 33, No. 3, January 18, 1990, pp. 173–177.
Mellor, Warren L., and P. Martin Hayden, "Issues and Channels in Communications Between a School and Its Parental Environment," *The Journal of Educational Administration*, Vol. 19, No. 1, Winter 1981.
Morgan, William R., "Learning and Student Life: Quality of Public and Private School Youth," *Sociology of Education*, Vol. 56, October 1983, pp. 187–202.
National Catholic Educational Association, *The Catholic High School: A National Portrait*, 1985.
National Commission on Excellence in Education, *A Nation at Risk: The Imperative for Educational Reform*, Washington, D.C., 1983.
New York City Board of Education, Office of Research, Evaluation, and Assessment, *Accountability Section Report: The Annual Dropout Rate 1987–88*, 1989.
Newmann, Fred M., "Student Engagement and High School Reform," *Educational Leadership*, February 1989.
Noell, Jay, "Public and Catholic Schools: A Reanalysis of 'Public and Private Schools,'" *Sociology of Education*, Vol. 55, April-July 1982, pp. 123–132.

Oakes, Jeannie, *Keeping Track*, Yale University Press, New Haven, 1985.
Ogbu, John U., "The Consequences of the American Caste System," in *The Achievement of Minority Students: New Perspectives*, U. Neisser (ed.), Lawrence Erlbaum, Hillsdale, New Jersey, 1986.
Perry, Imani, "A Black Student's Reflection on Public and Private Schools," *Harvard Educational Review*, Vol. 58, No. 3, August 1988, pp. 332–336.
Peters, Thomas J., and Robert H. Waterman, *In Search of Excellence*, Harper and Row, New York, 1982.
Powell, Arthur G., "Observations on the Discovery of Private Schools as a Subject for Educational Research," in Susan Abramowitz and E. Ann Stackhouse (eds.), *The Private High School Today*, National Institute of Education, Washington, D.C., December 1980.
Powell, Arthur G., Eleanor Farrar, and David K. Cohen, *The Shopping Mall High School*, Houghton Mifflin Company, Boston, 1985.
Ratski, Anne, "The Remarkable Impact of Creating a School Community: One Model of How It Can Be Done, An Interview," *American Educator*, Spring 1988, pp. 10–17, 38–43.
Rosenholtz, Susan J., "Effective Schools: Interpreting the Evidence," *American Journal of Education*, Vol. 93, No. 3, May 1985.
Schneider, Frank W., and Larry W. Coutts, "The High School Environment: A Comparison of Coeducational and Single-Sex Schools," *Journal of Educational Psychology*, Vol. 74, No. 6, 1982, pp. 898–906.
Sedlak, Michael W., Christopher W. Wheeler, Diana C. Pullin, and Philip A. Cusick, *Selling Students Short*, Teachers College Press, New York, 1986.
Selvin, M., et al., *Who Gets What and Why: Curriculum Decisionmaking at Three Comprehensive High Schools*, The RAND Corporation, Santa Monica, Calif., N-3041-NCRVE/UCB, February 1990.
Shanker, Albert, "The End of the Traditional Model of Schooling—And a Proposal for Using Incentives to Restructure Our Public Schools," *Phi Delta Kappan*, Vol. 71, No. 5, January 1990, pp. 344–357.
——, "Restructuring American Education," in *Roundtable on Urban Education*, Business-Higher Education Forum, Washington, D.C., 1989.
Sizer, Theodore R., *Horace's Compromise: The Dilemma of the American High School*, Houghton Mifflin Company, Boston, 1984.
Smith, Gerald R., Thomas B. Gregory, and Richard C. Pugh, "Meeting Student Needs: Evidence for the Superiority of Alternative

Schools," *Phi Delta Kappan*, Vol. 62, No. 8, April 1981, pp. 561–564.

State Education Department, *New York, The State of Learning: Statewide Profile of the Educational System*, Albany, New York, January 1, 1989.

Tomlinson, Tommy M., "The Troubled Years: An Interpretive Analysis of Public Schools Since 1950," *Phi Delta Kappan*, Vol. 62, No. 5, January 1981, pp. 371–377.

U.S. Department of Education, *American Education: Making it Work*, Washington, D.C., 1988.

Wise, Arthur E., *Legislated Learning*, University of California Press, Berkeley, Calif., 1979.

LC 3726 .H55 1990
Hill, Paul Thomas, 1943-
High schools with character

rescued 11/06
by Sharon Gibson

DATE DUE

2 7/10			
3/2/09			